CHEER

ALSO BY MIKE WOLF

Barantined: Recipes, Tips, and Stories to Enjoy at Home
Lost Spring: How We Cocktailed through Crisis
Garden to Glass: Grow Your Drinks from the Ground Up

JACK ROSE
p. 55

CHEER

A LIQUID GOLD HOLIDAY DRINKING GUIDE

MIKE WOLF

WITH KENNETH DEDMON, JESSICA BACKHUS,
& BRITTANY AUGUSTINE

TURNER
PUBLISHING COMPANY

Turner Publishing Company
Nashville, Tennessee
www.turnerpublishing.com

Cover design by Archie Ferguson Design
Book design by Stacy Wakefield Forte
Photography by Christine Souder
Illustrations by Jenna Pearl Leonard

Library of Congress Cataloging-in-Publication Data

Names: Wolf, Mike, 1980- author.
Title: Cheer : liquid gold holiday drinking guide / Mike Wolf with Kenneth
  Dedmon, Jessica Backhus, and Brittany Augustine.
Description: Nashville, Tennessee : Turner Publishing Company, [2022] |
  Includes index.
Identifiers: LCCN 2022017097 (print) | LCCN 2022017098 (ebook) | ISBN
  9781684425624 (hardcover) | ISBN 9781684425631 (paperback) | ISBN
  9781684425648 (epub)
Subjects: LCSH: Cocktails. | Holiday cooking. | LCGFT: Cookbooks.
Classification: LCC TX951 .W565 2022 (print) | LCC TX951 (ebook) | DDC
  641.87/4--dc23/eng/20211018
LC record available at https://lccn.loc.gov/2022017097
LC ebook record available at https://lccn.loc.gov/2022017098

Printed in the United States of America

THIS BOOK IS DEDICATED TO THE MEMORY
OF KATIE WOLF, MY GRANDMOTHER AND
CHAMPION OF WOMEN IN POLITICS.
SHE ALWAYS MADE CHRISTMAS SO SPECIAL
AT HER HOUSE.

AND FOR CHRIS, THE DOG AND
LIQUID GOLD MASCOT.

Contents

Holidaze

New Year, New Brews

VANHATTAN
p. 37

Tradition and Ritual

by Lisa Donovan

If you're lucky like I was, your childhood might be full of beautiful traditions centered around the holidays. My mother was masterful at setting a table for a holiday meal, filling it with casseroles and sticky sweet hams, usually deciding to stay with familiar recipes but trying a new one from her new issue of Southern Living if the inspiration struck. She took this task to heart and always kept me by her side.

There was this unbridled love inside of her, and this was her way of bringing it out and showing us. She grew up in an era where material things were the way you showed the people around you how you felt. For me—and maybe this is because of how special she would make Christmas—material things were never that important, so while it was easy to shower my two little ones with toys while they were young, it became different as they got a little older. As a parent, it started to get more difficult to figure out what they wanted, while watching them figure out their own personalities and who they're becoming as people. One of the traditions that I started when they became teenagers was to invest in individual experiences for each of them, where I could spend time with them alone in a way that I felt they would really enjoy. For Maggie, it was taking her to see the musical *Hamilton*. For Joseph, it was taking him to see Wilco in Chicago. I loved taking them to a new city and of course, the whole trip would become about food. We'd spend a few days in Chinatown eating the best dumplings or traverse the city seeking out the best tacos. For Maggie, it was finding the best deep-dish pizza in Chicago. I wanted to figure out how to give them things that I think are helping them become the people they want to become and sharing new experiences with them. So that has become our Christmas tradition. I try to think about experiences they would want to have, and I make it happen. Outside of the idea of gift-giving, food and drink are always what the holidays are centered around. Since I don't cook as much on a day-to-day basis anymore, the holidays have become a really important time to be in the kitchen making things for the people I love.

Over the last few years with a global pandemic, we were forced to not see each other for long periods of time. Though difficult for many families, I found some relief in that. The willingness to say, "I don't want to do that anymore," can be powerful. The holidays can have a lot of pressure, especially if you're the family who lives apart from the rest of your family. You're supposed to pack everything up, drive for hours, stay in a weird motel, all with your emotions running high. It's not exactly restful, and it takes us away from our own rituals. Not traditions, but rituals. Sometimes when you're so busy during the holidays trying to please everyone in your whole family, you lose sight of the rituals of your immediate family, whether that's your children, your friends, or your support system. Now that my kids are older, it's enough of an orchestration just to get them to come home for the holidays. Focusing on ritual and not necessarily tradition, really helped our family find our rhythm over the last few years in a way that we never had. Watching my kids relax and sink into themselves for a few days is a real gift. The last few years has given us permission to see that the easy thing might be the healthy thing rather than the lazy thing. The book you hold in your hands gives you so much permission to let loose and make punches, cocktails and batches of beautiful drinks. The Thanksgiving section alone covers so much ground and makes me excited for that special time of year. I also love how old school many of these ideas are. There are Champagne cocktails, old fashioneds, and martinis, batched for an entire party.

No matter what will happen when you throw a holiday party, people are going to gravitate to the kitchen. It just happens that way. Don't forget to enjoy yourself and not put yourself in a position where you're uncomfortable, or spending too much time away from your guests, unless that's your goal. The kitchen can either be a place where you're furiously trying to catch up on all of your sides or drinks, or it can be a place to hide away for a few minutes. Shit, that's why I started cooking in the first place. When you're planning out a gathering, the second you begin to feel anxiety or pressure about a given dish or drink, just don't do it. It's lovely to impress people, but it's way more impressive when the host is present, whole and offering whatever they have to the people they love. People want to walk into warmth, and hospitality doesn't mean doing the most fancy thing. Spend your money on good quality ingredients, but don't go overboard on the most expensive stuff you can find. Set a table with anything you have growing in your yard. It's sweet, charming as fuck, and really heartfelt. If I walk into someone's house and I see the table set with something I saw growing outside, I feel a little more at home. Grab some leaves from the lawn outside and make it look pretty. None of it has to be a burden to you, and the less of a burden it is to you, the more enjoyable it will be to your guests. If you hand someone a glass of wine and they say, "How can I help?" If you need it, give them something to do so you feel less overwhelmed and can share in that moment. Let it be a place of joy and fulfillment, not stress and anxiety.

This fine book you hold in your hands gives you so much permission to let loose, settle in and make punches, cocktails and batches of beautiful drinks that encourage this kind of revelry and togetherness. I love recipes with stories and I love the way Mike always connects these ideas of human connection to his work. He brings old school ideas like Champagne cocktails, old fashioned's, and martinis, to the forefront and also gives you the confidence to batch up a recipe for an entire party.

I know you will find so many good recipes to dive into to make new traditions and rituals for yourself and your family and your friends in this book. Try one, try them all. Don't pass the classic Eggnog recipe by, of which there are many. It is the perfect example of holiday drinking. It's cream, eggs and rich with alcohol. When else is there a time when this is okay to take on such a rich indulgence other than the holidays? Eggnog is like a distillation of one of my only rules this time of year: spend your money on quality ingredients. Use the good, local cream, buy the best eggs you can find, and don't forget to use the nice cognac, if you can afford it. I'll add here the one drink that sums up the holidays for me: Cheatham County Artillery Punch. Every year for New Year's Day, I host a "Peas and Greens Hangover Brunch," and I make the biggest batch of this punch I can afford, a revived old recipe from the 1870s here in Tennessee. It is delicious and far too easy to drink. Warn your guests, encourage them to take it slow, have a couch they can sleep on if necessary. I tell everyone "Have one cup now and see how you feel in an hour." It is my go-to for Mardi Gras, and it's great for a New Year's celebration. I hope it brings you cheer.

Cheatham County Artillery Punch

16 lemons

4 oranges

1 pound sugar

1 750 ml bottle of Bourbon or Rye

1 750 ml bottle of Cognac or Brandy

1 750 ml bottle of Dark Jamaican rum

3 bottles of Sparkling wine

Garnish: Shaved nutmeg and slices of lemons

Begin by peeling the fruit of 16 lemons and 4 oranges and put the peels into a bowl. Juice enough lemons to get a pint of juice, strained. Add the sugar to the bowl of lemon and orange peels and gently muddle to incorporate the sugar. Let the zest and sugar sit on a countertop for a few hours to draw out the oil. After a few hours, muddle the peels and sugar some more and add the lemon juice. Muddle and then stir the lemon juice to dissolve the rest of the sugar. Strain this mixture into your punch bowl (straining out the peels). Add the three bottles of booze and stir to combine. Now your punch is ready to party. Before serving time, fill the punch bowl with ice and stir everything together over ice. Add the sparkling wine, shave some nutmeg over the top, and you're ready to serve.

**APPLE
ORANGE
COLLINS**
p. 52

Liquid Gold for the Holidaze

Drinking season—the period that begins with the first chill in the air in September, and stretches on through to New Year's Eve—begins contemplatively, with a glass of whiskey or full-bodied red wine, slowly building to a bubbly, celebratory cheer when the year, with all its failures, disappointments, triumphs, and treasures, is finally over.

Rebirth, after the inevitable hangover (don't worry, we've got you covered there too), is right around the corner. A new year begins, we hunker down, embrace healthier habits along with a hermitic lifestyle, until mid-January or so when we're ready to break free and get back out in the world. "Don't threaten me with a good time" becomes "Please give me an excuse to cheat a little on my resolutions." Or maybe we just crave human interaction. In the Before Times, we came together to celebrate many things: birthdays, anniversaries, graduations, weddings, and of course holidays. But we also shared a spirit of togetherness at sporting events, concerts, festivals, happy hour with the work crew, even the release of a new beer down at the local brewery. It is this spirit of comradery, friendship, and common ground that we've been missing for so long, from which Liquid Gold was born. Co-author Kenneth Dedmon and I, veteran barmen who had worked together for six-plus years, were having separation anxiety as I left the famed Husk bar in Nashville that I had opened and run as bar manager for the previous five years. I was moving on to start new projects, open a tiki bar, and write a book, which became *Garden to Glass: Grow Your Drinks from the Ground Up.* Kenneth faithfully remained at Husk, entertaining guests by regaling them with half-truths from his upbringing in Nashville, or breaking down exactly why they needed a pour of $52 thirteen-year-old rye whiskey at that precise moment. We missed the laughs and sense of accomplishment of getting through a busy Saturday without breaking anything, or asking some tourist from Florida "Are you wearing socks right now?" We also missed entertaining our friends from the industry—whiskey distillers, reps from all stripes, brewers, bartenders, and cocktail lovers. So, we did what any other disconnected member of society would do: we started a podcast.

The name Liquid Gold, like many great drinks and recipes, began with a mistake. One day while tasting through different cider varieties, I did my impersonation of the weasel from Wes Anderson's Thanksgiving classic "Fantastic Mr. Fox," voiced by Willem Dafoe. "Like pure, liquid gold," I said, tasting through some of the newer varieties of Foggy Ridge's award-winning cider (featured on page 45). Later that night, I put together a cocktail to commemorate the fact that I was now calling everything "liquid gold," from the Moscato-laced, delightful vermouth known as Cocchi Americano (with the gold foil wrapping) to the incomparable "pear in a bottle brandy" from Clear Creek Distillers in Oregon (page 69) that we proudly displayed on the back bar. Here's the gist of the recipe:

The Liquid Gold Cocktail

1 oz. Cocchi Americano vermouth

1 oz. Clear Creek Pear Brandy (pear in a bottle version, for more see page 73)

½ oz. Foggy Ridge Pippen Gold Dessert Cider (no longer available; substitute Sauternes or another dessert wine)

4 oz. light, dry cider such as Brightwood Cider

Stir the first three ingredients together in a mixing glass with plenty of ice until thoroughly chilled. Strain into a coupe glass and top with the cider. Garnish with an apple slice and a lemon twist.

It was only later, when I was watching the film for the fifty-seventh time with my son Henry, that I realized the treacherous Weasel hadn't even said "liquid gold." In the scene, after battling it out with the Fantastic Fox, who steps in to save his son from the villainous weasel, Mr. Fox reaches down to the dying, defeated Weasel lying on the brick floor of the sewer. "Here's a beaker of Bean's finest cider," he says, giving the weasel a handful of sewer water as he takes his last breath. "Like pure, melted gold," says the weasel before his eyes cross and he drifts off to weasel heaven. Either way, Liquid Gold stuck.

LIQUID
GOLD
COCKTAIL
p. 15

When it came time to invite our first guest and stroll into the studios at the We Own This Town Podcast Network, it was the holiday season of 2018 and I was armed with recipes. The Eggnog and Whiskey Cream I had been making at Husk for years (always a secret—shhh don't tell) were thrust out into the open as we gave recipes, techniques, and even recipes to follow up on using those techniques. We felt a weight off our shoulders as, week after week, we'd divulge all the tricks of the trade, the secrets bartenders only tell each other in the waning hours before closing time at someone else's bar. Maybe they weren't secrets, after all. Making and enjoying beverages of all kinds is a timeless art where knowledge expands like the universe.

We'd love for you to take this book and make a mess of it. "Buy two, in fact! Put one on your coffee table and one in your kitchen," says Kenneth in his wry, marketing-savvy rasp. Take these recipes and use them as templates to build your own unique flavors. Pay attention to the ratios and the methods more than the brands used or the products we tout. There are Booze News anecdotes peppered throughout the book, meant to inform, entertain, and give your family something to talk about while you're busy making food and drinks. Jessica Backhus, our Cocktail Correspondent on the show, offers plenty of advice for planning out your holiday party, along with wine-pairing notes (page 253) and tips for making the ideal "Italian Grandpa" cocktail, whatever that is. We also have a primer on throwing your very own "Harry Potter Cocktail Party," from Liquid Gold Potions Master, Brittany Augustine (page 304). There are even a few fiction short stories for you to duck into when the crowd is gone and you're feeling festive. What follows are stories about the drinks we love and how they're shaped by the people we love. Hell, sometimes we even drink them to simply get through being around the people we love. This book is about the time after the first chill of the year, when we realize that the warmth we seek in our glass isn't as important as the people that we share those moments with. To our comrades in bars, families at home, families far gone, and familial customs that have turned into memories-passed-on, let's raise a glass. It's time for the liquid gold cheer:

To heck with the past, we pour a little out for all the people who have passed, while we look to the future to appreciate and enjoy what's in our glass. May we put our differences aside and realize we all want the same thing: to love and be loved, to embrace humanity and be connected, even if just for one night. So let's drink up before the season passes, and we wake up hung over, looking like asses.

The
First
Chill in
the Air

LINCOLN
COUNTY
COCKTAIL
p. 23

Whiskey Drinks by the Fire, with Friends

How to begin a holiday book
about booze? With lumps of charcoal,
of course!

Over the years, much has been made about how to define "Tennessee Whiskey." When Kenneth and I were bartending at Husk together, we even had a reporter from CNN who came in to get a quote about why Tennessee whiskey was special or different from bourbon. Is it merely whiskey that's made in Tennessee? Now, that would be too easy for a business built on myth, magical marketing, nostalgia, and history. Does it have to be made in Lynchburg, home of Jack Daniels and, more recently, Uncle Nearest Distillery? You're getting warmer. Is it just bourbon that isn't made in Kentucky? Well, sort of. What makes a Tennessee whiskey a true Tennessee Whiskey isn't just that it was distilled, aged, and bottled in Tennessee: it's that the whiskey was filtered through sugar maple charcoal, known as the "Lincoln County Process." What this apparently does for the taste of the whiskey is debatable. Originally used as a means to filter out impurities for a smoother, easy-drinking product, today's burly higher-proof whiskies would have left the likes of George Dickel, Jack Daniels, and Charles Nelson—the original Tennessee whiskey triumvirate who agreed on this method of production in the first place—bemused, wondering, "Why are y'all so interested in all this higher-proof lightning water? You tryin' to start a fire?"

I sat down around a blazing fire and asked Charlie Nelson, great-great-great-grandson of whiskey baron Charles Nelson, and one of the key players in the revival of this category of whiskey, why it was important to keep Tennessee whiskey separate from bourbon. Charlie even went before the state legislature in Tennessee to speak on the matter, years before relaunching his family whiskey back into the world.

"I spent a lot of time researching my family's history and looking at old newspaper articles that talked about the distinction of this whiskey," Charlie said. "My great-great-great-grandfather Charles Nelson was a pioneer for Tennessee whiskey, and there were all these old articles talking about the difference between Tennessee whiskey and bourbon. Some of these articles talked about the charcoal-mellowing having a positive impact on the aging process, that a charcoal-filtered whiskey would come to maturity much faster than a bourbon. Above all, it made for a smoother whiskey."

Try these smooth, easy-drinking cocktails at your next bonfire or backyard get-together.

Lincoln County Cocktail

¼ oz. Maple-Smoked Maple Syrup (recipe follows)

2 dashes aromatic bitters

1 thin piece of lemon peel, as little pith as possible

2 oz. Nelson's Greenbrier Tennessee Whiskey

Garnish: slice of apple

In a mixing glass, lightly muddle the lemon peel with the maple syrup and bitters. Add the whiskey and plenty of ice and stir until the drink is well chilled. Strain into an old-fashioned glass over a big ice cube or two and garnish with an apple slice. Enjoy by a fire.

Maple-Smoked Maple Syrup

2 cups maple syrup

1 cup water

Plastic wrap, enough to completely cover the pot you're making the syrup in

1 large chunk (about the size of a baseball) of burning maple charcoal, or other hardwood like hickory (use tongs and make it outside, dummy)

Prepare a fire outdoors, using sugar maple if you're able to, or another hardwood like hickory. Combine the maple syrup and water in a saucepan or pot by heating and stirring to incorporate the ingredients. Once your fire is burning pretty well and you've got a foundation of embers keeping it roiling, take your tongs and grab a baseball-sized piece of burning charcoal. Have your plastic wrap ready to cover the pot of syrup immediately. Drop the ember in the syrup and, using a quick but light hand, cover the pot and trap in the smoke. Let the syrup and ember sit together smoking for 45 minutes. If, after 45 minutes, you don't have a smoky flavor to your liking, try to "wrap and trap" another ember and steep it for another 45 minutes to an hour. When the flavor is right, strain out the embers, bottle, and store your syrup in the refrigerator. It will keep for at least 2 months.

Batched Lincoln County Cocktail

Serves 6

3 oz. Maple-Smoked Maple Syrup

12 dashes aromatic bitters

6 thin pieces of lemon peel, as little pith as possible

6 oz. water

12 oz. Nelson's Greenbrier Tennessee Whiskey

Garnish: slices of apple

In a large mixing glass or bowl, lightly muddle the lemon peels with the maple syrup and bitters. Add the whiskey and water and stir or whisk to combine. Bottle the batch or place into a container with a lid in the refrigerator. When it comes time to serve, pour over ice, and garnish with a slice of apple. Enjoy by a fire.

THE GATEWAY DRINK

If you're planning on having a bonfire or any autumnal gathering of like-minded whiskey drinkers, it's always a good idea to have some vodka or tequila lying around for those unfortunate souls who don't drink whiskey. There's also a way to present whiskey in a more approachable light, less old-fashionedy and more Lynchburg lemonade style. There are plenty of dynamic, accessible flavors that also go really well with whiskey that you can use to craft a crowd-pleasing whiskey concoction. Before we get into a cocktail equivalent of a "gateway drink," here are some flavors to keep in mind when introducing anyone to the joys of whiskey:

+ Ginger, with its spicy bite and lifting aroma, can help compete with any astringency or intensity of whiskey for a newbie.

+ Lemon helps to cut the round sweetness of many bourbons and goes well with many of whiskey's other flavor affinities, like the aforementioned ginger.

+ Stone fruits such as peaches and apricots work really well when mixed with bourbon. Add some lemon for acidity and you're smack-dab on a porch on a summer day.

+ Water can really open up the flavor profile and aroma of a good whiskey. If you're making a simple old-fashioned for a new-to-whiskey friend, try adding an ounce to an ounce and a half of water in the glass to introduce these big flavors in a lighter way.

The Gateway Drink

6 lemon verbena leaves, divided

1 dash Fee's Whiskey Barrel Bitters

Pinch of Maldon sea salt

2 oz. Belle Meade Bourbon

½ oz. apricot liqueur, Rothman and Winter

½ oz. Grilled Peach Cordial (recipe follows)

½ oz. fresh lemon juice

Spritzes of Chamomile Tincture (recipe follows)

Combine 5 of the verbena leaves, the bitters, and the sea salt in a shaker and muddle. Add the bourbon, liqueur, cordial, and lemon juice, fill the shaker halfway with ice, and shake vigorously until well chilled. Strain into a rocks glass, spray a few times with the tincture, garnish with the remaining verbena leaf, and serve.

Grilled Peach Cordial

1½ cups sugar

⅔ cup water

1 teaspoon distilled white vinegar

½ teaspoon ground cinnamon

2 large ripe peaches (about 8 oz.), cut away from the pit and into quarters

1½ teaspoons grated orange zest (use a Microplane)

Combine the sugar and water in a small saucepan and bring the mixture to a simmer over medium heat, stirring to dissolve the sugar, about 5 minutes. Remove from the stove and cool to room

temperature. Add the vinegar and cinnamon and stir to combine. Transfer to a container or jar and set aside.

Prepare a hot grill, distributing the coals in an even layer in the bottom of the grill.

Place the peaches in the grill basket cut side down, and place the basket directly on the coals. Grill the peach quarters until they develop a dark char, about 3 minutes. Turn the peaches and cook on the other side until lightly charred, another 2 minutes. Transfer the peaches to the container of syrup, add the orange zest, cover, and let the cordial cool to room temperature. Then place in the refrigerator and infuse overnight.

Strain the cordial through a fine-mesh sieve into a clean container and discard the solids. Cover and refrigerate. Tightly covered, the cordial will keep for up to 2 weeks in the refrigerator.

Chamomile Tincture

Makes 1 cup

2 cups fresh chamomile flowers

1 tablespoon dried chamomile flowers

1 cup 100-proof vodka

Combine all the ingredients in a clean pint canning jar, wipe the rim and threads clean, place the lid and ring on, tighten the ring, and store the tincture in a cool, dark place for at least 2 weeks, shaking the mixture every other day, to infuse the tincture.

Strain the tincture through a fine-mesh sieve lined with cheesecloth into a clean pint canning jar and discard the solids. Wipe the rim and threads clean, place the lid and ring on, tighten the ring, and store the tincture at room temperature. It will keep for at least 4 months.

Gateway Drink, Simplified for a Gathering

Half gallon (64 oz.) peach iced tea

12 lemon verbena or lemon balm leaves (optional)

2 bags chamomile tea

6 dashes aromatic bitters

1 teaspoon sea salt

12 oz. bourbon

2 oz. apricot liqueur

1 oz. Grilled Peach Cordial (optional, substitute simple syrup)

½ cup lemon juice

Garnish: lemon wheels; mint

In a large pitcher or punch bowl, combine the peach tea, lemon herbs, and chamomile tea bags and stir to combine and release some flavor from the tea and herbs. Infuse in the refrigerator for an hour, or two hours for a stronger flavor. Strain out the lemon herbs and take out the tea bags. Add the bitters, salt, bourbon, Apricot Liqueur, peach syrup, and lemon juice and whisk to combine. Taste for desired sweetness and serve over ice. Garnish with lemon wheels and mint.

OL' SORGY AND
THE VANHATTAN

When I was running the bar at Husk, I needed a drink that could epitomize the distinctive flavors of the South while quelling the insatiable thirst for bourbon that our customers had in 2013 (at press time, the bourbon boom shows no signs of slowing down). Since sorghum was to be a pantry staple and a common ingredient for the pastry chefs to use, I started getting familiar with its dark, rich, grassy, corn-flakes-and-dark-honey-flavor profile. To my delight, it was amazing with bourbon, and you didn't need much sorghum for the marriage to make sense. Since both products—the bourbon and the sorghum—came from Kentucky, there was a symbiotic flavor affinity that made for liquid magic. We had a lot of wheated bourbon lying around, and the soft spice imparted by the wheat in the bourbon lent itself well to the rich texture of the sorghum.

On the first night we were open, Julian Van Winkle—steward of the vaunted Pappy Van Winkle bourbon label and grandson of Pappy himself—plopped down in a barstool at the corner pocket of the L-shaped bar in the grand antebellum house on Rutledge Hill in Nashville. Our first full order of liquor wouldn't arrive until a few days later, so we had limited offerings. As it turned out, there was indeed Pappy Van Winkle bourbon lying around somewhere under the floorboards, but none of us knew about it at that point. We did, however, have some Buffalo Trace bourbon available that night (we would receive a delivery of sixty different bourbons later in the week, just the beginning), which suited Julian just fine since his family whiskey was now distilled and aged under the tutelage of Buffalo Trace. Located in Frankfort, Kentucky, a capital city resting on a double bend in the Kentucky River fifty-five miles southeast of Louisville, Buffalo Trace produces much of the most sought-after bourbon in the world.

"What can I get for you tonight?" I asked Julian, who probably had a hip flask of whiskey in his pocket filled with bourbon worth thousands of dollars.

"Buffalo Trace will be just fine tonight, Mike," he said with an easy smile and a laid-back attitude. Now came the moment of truth.

"How do you like it? Neat?" I asked, not wanting to suggest he have it any other way.

"On the rocks with a lemon twist would be perfect," he said, much to my surprise. "That's how I love all my whiskey. Have you tried my rye? It's tough to get your hands on. Sometimes even I can't get it," he said with a chuckle.

I started to ask more about the lemon twist itself, which was fascinating to me. One of the most distinguished whiskey tasters and professionals in the world actually preferred a garnish? I loved it. Here was a guy who appreciated and understood the finer things in life. It was then that I knew any garnish we'd use for the in-development sorghum old-fashioned would have to include a lemon twist of some sort. Julian seemed like a cocktail guy to me now, so I asked him what his favorite cocktail was.

"Has Sean (Brock) ever told you about the Vanhattan?" he asked, with a twinkle in his eye.

"I don't believe so," I said. I mean, Chef Brock had told me a million things in the weeks leading up to Husk's opening, like what a benne seed was (African descendant of the sesame seed, a forgotten ingredient in Southern cuisine), what was so special about ramps (god's gift to cooking was creating the perfect blend of garlic and onion, just asking for pork fat), and the magic of pure Tennessee Valley buttermilk ("It's the best shit in the building," Brock would say).

"Well, what I like about the Vanhattan is it has both bourbon and rye," he began, "and it's so strong you don't need to get your ass off the couch to make another one for a while." *Sold*, I thought. I asked for the recipe, and he politely obliged, a true Southern gentleman. Some details, such as the sweet vermouth (he suggested Carpano Antica), seemed vague at first, but since I was right in front of him, I could use my jigger to show him how the measurements looked. We wrote it down on receipt paper directly on the dark, textured leather-granite bar top, and I can still remember how jagged the handwriting looked. We thought we might frame it, but instead we stashed it under the cash drawer for safekeeping. It stayed there for years, and even showed up on menus from time to time. It's a bold, nuanced, delicious "couch drink" if there ever was one.

As for the "Ol' Sorgy" cocktail, it would become a smash hit. It became so popular that the two bartenders behind the bar would each be making three at a time. It began outselling draft beer in droves, so we got rid of the beer taps and were suddenly making a lot of cocktails. For our regulars, we even started making a few Vanhattans.

Ol' Sorgy

One thin lemon peel, as little pith as possible

Scant ¼ oz. sorghum syrup** (1 part sorghum to 1 part water)

2 dashes aromatic bitters

2 oz. bourbon (Medley Bros. would be a great choice)

Garnish: orange peel

At the bottom of a mixing glass, lightly muddle (as in cajole, persuade, caress) the citrus peel, along with the bitters and the sorghum syrup, before adding the ice. Then add the bourbon and the ice, and stir until well chilled. Pour over a big ice cube or two in an old-fashioned glass, and garnish with an orange or lemon peel, expressed over the top of the glass.

**For the sorghum syrup, add a jar of sorghum to a saucepan and use a spatula to dislodge as much of the sorghum from the jar as possible. Then fill the jar up with warm water and—again, using the spatula—stir the water and dislodge all the sorghum from the jar before pouring the water into the saucepan. Simmer over medium-low heat for 20 minutes. Bottle and keep in the refrigerator. The syrup will keep for a few months, much longer if you add an ounce of vodka or whiskey.

Batched
Ol' Sorgy

Serves 6

4 thin strips of orange peel, as little pith as possible

4 thin strips of lemon peel, as little pith as possible

2¾ oz. sorghum syrup** (1 part sorghum to 1 part water)

6 oz. water

12 dashes aromatic bitters

12 oz. bourbon (preferably something with a proof in the 100 range)

Garnish: lemon peels; sprigs of thyme

In a large mixing glass or bowl, lightly muddle (as in cajole, persuade, caress) the strips of citrus peel, along with the bitters and the sorghum syrup. Then add the bourbon and water, and stir to incorporate. Bottle this mixture, or store in a container with a lid in the refrigerator. To serve, pour over ice and garnish with a lemon peel and a sprig of thyme. Use the batched cocktail within a month.

Vanhattan

1½ oz. rye whiskey

1½ oz. bourbon

½ oz. Carpano Antica sweet vermouth

2 dashes Stirrings Blood Orange bitters

1 dash Angostura bitters

1 teaspoon Luxardo Maraschino cherry syrup (the syrup that's preserving the cherries in the jar)

Combine the whiskey, bourbon, vermouth, bitters, and cherry syrup in a mixing glass full of ice and stir for a good 20 seconds or so. Let the drink sit in the mixing glass undisturbed for 5 minutes. Serve over a big ice cube and garnish with a lemon or orange peel, expressed and twisted into the glass. Also garnish with cherries, if desired. Find a couch to sit on.

3 MORE OF OUR FAVORITE WHISKEY DRINKS

Brooklyn

2 oz. bourbon or rye whiskey

¾ oz. sweet vermouth

¼ oz. Bigallet China China or Amaro Ciao Caro (2 spirits that are most similar to Amer Picon, which is no longer available)

1 dash aromatic bitters

Garnish: orange peel

Stir ingredients in a mixing glass with plenty of ice until thoroughly chilled. Strain into a coupe glass and garnish with an orange twist or orange peel, expressed and discarded.

Scotch Toddy

1 black tea bag or tea of your choice

1½ oz. blended scotch

½ oz. honey syrup (one part honey to one part water)

1 dash Angostura or cinnamon bitters (page 116)

Tiny pinch of salt

Garnish: 1 orange wedge

Begin by boiling enough water for twice the amount of drinks that you're making. When the water is ready, pour enough into your mug to temper it so it keeps warm for the duration of your drink. Placing a small plate or bowl over the top of the mug can help retain the heat as well. Once the mug is fully hot and ready for action, discard the tempering water and make the tea by pouring more water, adding the tea bag, and covering the mug for maximum extraction.

After 3 to 4 minutes of brew time, set aside the tea bag (for your next hot toddy) and add the scotch, honey, bitters, and tiny bit of salt. Squeeze a few drops of orange over the top and garnish with the orange wedge. Thyme, rosemary, and sage would make for aroma-boosting garnishes as well.

Rob Roy

2 oz. of your favorite scotch

¾ oz. sweet vermouth

1 barspoon orange curacao

2 dashes of Angostura or cinnamon bitters (page 116)

Tiny pinch of salt

Garnish: orange peel; dehydrated orange slice

Fill a mixing glass with ice, and add scotch, vermouth, orange curacao, bitters, and salt. Stir briskly for 15 seconds until well chilled. Let sit for 4 to 5 minutes until very cold and serve up in a coupe glass or in an old-fashioned glass with a large ice cube. Garnish with an orange peel expressed over the top of the drink, or a dehydrated orange peel.

86 THE 86

In 2002, like a ninja, Jack Daniels diluted the bottling of Old No. 7 from 86 to 80 proof. Over a year later, celebrating Frank Sinatra's birthday, my roommates purchased a bottle. Nearly halfway through the bottle, we noticed the slight change to the label. There was no uproar among the four of us, we just drank faster and joked about it around a campfire. On many nights like that night, we would write songs, and these are all the lyrics I can remember from that session:

> Jack D, you S O B,
> You took some whiskey
> away from me.
> What you did makes me feel sick.
> Why did you 86 the 86?

Something happened in the ensuing years in the whiskey industry. After a slow decline in demand, sales began to crescendo. In 2006, the Kentucky bourbon industry was valued at $800 million based on total volume. That value increased 20 percent in 2007, as people became enamored with all things bourbon. By 2013, the estimated value of ricked bourbon (whiskey that was resting in the barrel) was over $1.5 billion. In seven years, the industry doubled in scope. The craft beer boom had already exploded, and morning shows were touting the idea of farm-to-table fine dining. The martini slowly slipped off the menu, and martini bars began to disappear.

In 2013, Maker's Mark Bourbon announced plans to drop their signature proof from 45 percent to 42 percent ABV, the same reduction of overall ABV as Jack Daniels's 86-to-80-proof move. Though it was more transparent, the Maker's Mark customer base responded to the change with outrage. Apologetic and appreciative, ownership abandoned their plan within a week. Both companies intended to cut costs and meet demand. It appears that Jack Daniels did it at a more opportune time, before the boom.

WHISKEY AND WIND IN WYOMING

There is one thing I have never been able to shake: my hatred for the wind. That is why I could never live in Wyoming, where the wind is not your friend. It feels like a bully holding you to the ground. Casper, Wyoming, is the state's second-largest city and the third-windiest, with an average wind speed of 12 mph. That sounds decent, right? No, it's not, because for every moment there is no wind, there is another where a violent gust of wind knocks you on your back. It is common for a gust to cause automobiles to swerve. To live there, you must be tough. Some even go insane.

On a Monday evening in early October 2017, Casper Police were alerted to a disturbance at a residence around 10 p.m. It was there that they found a wobbly Bryant Johnson, with a story I wish were true. Demanding to speak to the town's "President," he claimed to be from the year 2048. He had time-traveled, using alien technology, warning "the aliens were coming next year and we needed to make sure to leave as fast as possible." Responding officers noted that he had slurred speech and a heavy alcohol stench. Bryant responded that it was part of the time-travel process: the aliens had injected him with alcohol before placing him in the time-travel device, described as a "giant pad." However, there had been a mistake, he claimed. He had overshot by one year, and the invasion was scheduled for the year 2018. With a blood alcohol level of .136, Bryant was transported to the Natrona County Detention Center. The time-travel device was never found.

SAVE THE WOMEN AND CHILDREN, DRINK THE WHISKEY

The last person known to have had a foot on the sinking ocean liner *Titanic* was Charles Joughin, an English-born baker and rarely documented hero of Liquid Gold lore. Depicted somewhat accurately in the James Cameron movie, Joughin spent many of the last hours of the *Titanic's* fateful descent distributing food to lifeboats, even giving up his space on one as an example to other male mariners, who were encouraged to save the women and children first. He did this all while consuming huge amounts of the whiskey that was very much at his disposal. Joughin threw deck chairs into the freezing water to be used as flotation devices for those too unlucky to find room on lifeboats, and claimed to have stepped into the ocean directly from the vessel as it was sinking, barely getting his hair wet. He attributed his survival to the amount of alcohol he had consumed as this tragedy transpired, keeping his blood warm enough as he waded and waited for rescue.

KENTUCKY DELUXE: IT'S A LIFESTYLE

Kentucky Deluxe is probably the cheapest whiskey you can possibly purchase for consumption in North America. Made by Heaven Hill, in Bardstown, Kentucky, it retails for around $10 per liter and usually remains in the brown bag after leaving the liquor store. Made from a blend of 20 percent bourbon and 80 percent unaged neutral grain spirit, it is the well whiskey of many dusty, smoke-encrusted taverns with broken pool tables on the outskirts of town. [A note from Mike: "At a honky-tonk I used to play outside of Fort Collins, we could have as much Kentucky Deluxe as we wanted throughout our set, but had to pay for everything else."]

It was right outside Oklahoma City where Kentucky Deluxe solidified itself as a garage-gargling juice of criminals of all repute. When Stephen Jennings was pulled over by Guthrie police officers, they (unbeknownst to them, who no doubt have no taste for even shitty whiskey) smelled the raw lightning of this spirit on Jennings's breath. While the car he was driving had been reported stolen, officers were shocked to find a terrarium with a live pet rattlesnake in the back. As the investigation developed, officers found a gun in the glove box with a half-empty bottle of Kentucky Deluxe. As if this traffic stop by the trailer park couldn't get stranger, police also found a container of powdered uranium in the car.

Mr. Jennings was booked for possession of a firearm with a felony record, possession of a stolen vehicle, suspended license, and an open container of Kentucky Deluxe. Mr. Jennings pointed out that the uranium was purchased legally in some states, even on Amazon! Mr. Jennings also eluded charges for the rattlesnake, due to his Oklahoma fishing and hunting license, allowing him to be in possession of certain pet wildlife. To this day, Heaven Hill has never commented on any crime involving Kentucky Deluxe.

STRANGER THAN FICTION, BUT STILL TRUE

On November 14, 2014, in the city of Gray, Louisiana, a man named Jack Daniels Leathers and his wife, Lydia, gave birth to a healthy baby boy they named Jim Beam. Mr. Daniels Leathers told the *Guardian* in the UK that he had been named Jack Daniels by his parents to upset the grandparents. Jack was merely paying it forward. He said if he was lucky enough to have another boy some day, he would name him Evan Williams, after the popular bourbon. The whiskey wonderment doesn't stop there, however. The happy couple's wedding was officiated by none other than Terrebonne Parish judge Johnny Walker.

TWO

Orchard-Based Cider, Apple Brandy, and Orchard Cocktails

I didn't know what "craft cider" was until I tried the award-winning ciders of Diane Flynt's Foggy Ridge Cidery, located in Dugspur, Virginia, near the Blue Ridge Parkway.

There was nothing angry about this orchard. Her ciders had structure, a light effervescence similar to the pet-nat that the cool dude at the wine shop just recommended to you, and, in the right light, constituted the visual representation of liquid gold. I didn't know I had been looking for a wizard who could turn old heirloom apple varieties into something that resembled a lighter, more delicate champagne; but here it was, dancing around my tongue and firing off receptors that said "I need more of this." I was hooked, and began pairing these lovely ciders with everything from pork chops and swordfish to Diane's favorite pairing, spicy brick-oven pizza. There was even a dessert cider, Pippin Gold, like a luscious apple cousin to Sauternes, amazing with foie gras, cheese, buttermilk pie, and cheesecake. A whole world of craft cider was suddenly opening up to me, and part of the sheer joy of it all was that most of these ciders reside in the neighborhood of 7 percent alcohol—half of most wines—so I began quoting a phrase borrowed from Spanish cider culture, as told to me by Cocktail Correspondent Jessica Backhus on the show "Don't Sip the Cider!" Then, at the top of her game, Ms. Flynt hung up the apple press for a full-time focus on the orchard itself.

Diane and her husband, Chuck, shuttered their cider-making oper-ation in late 2018—they changed the world, what else do you want from them?—though they are still maintaining the plethora of heirloom apple varieties and redoubling their efforts to educate consumers, orchardists, and cider brewers about the importance of cider apples. No Grannies (Smiths) allowed. The crux of what Flynt is looking for in an apple is tannin, due to the complexity that it brings when pressed, fermented, and turned into cider. Many of these older varieties go back to a time when America was in its infancy as a country, with one of her variet-ies, Hewe's Virginia Crab, grafted from the orchards at Mount Vernon, where George Washington used to make cider, back when it was safer and more popular than water. I asked Diane specifically what it meant to make "orchard-based" cider and why the varieties that she has spent over two decades bringing to life are so important.

"I think of it as two tracks running alongside each other," said Diane. "You have the varieties of apples, and the way they are grown. If you think along the lines of how grapes are turned into wine, you can take any old grape—say a green concord grape sitting on your table—and make wine with it, but it's not going to have the same character and depth of flavor as if you had made wine with a Chardonnay grape or Petite Verdot or any other great wine grape. The same is true with apples. You can make cider with a Granny Smith apple or a red delicious, but it's not going to have the same depth of flavor and be nearly as delicious as if you had made the cider with a Dabbonet, or a Hewe's Crab Apple. The components you're looking for in a cider apple are the same that you look for in a wine grape. You want tannin, acid, sugar, and complex flavor. And you don't have those elements in the apples you buy at the grocery store or even many farm stands."

She's passionate about the way the orchard is farmed, and can now turn her attention away from the pressing of the apples to the complexities of the growing seasons in Appalachia at over 3,000 feet.

"You've got to pay attention to how these apples are grown and harvested. Many apples are grown and harvested on large-scale farms for the purpose of long-storing them. They'll go into cold storage, or into a controlled-atmosphere storage, and they're going to be hanging around for months and months. They're not harvesting ripe fruit, and the flavor has not developed. At our orchard, we harvest apples like a vineyard harvests grapes. We're out every day, testing and tasting apples to make sure the flavor is developing before we harvest. There really is terroir when it comes to apples in the same way we hear that term used for grapes in the wine world. Many of the old Southern varieties of apples that we grow here at this elevation taste very different than when they come from the Shenandoah Valley or down in North Carolina."

Now, I'm a romantic guy, especially when it comes to food and beverage, so all this talk of terroir, agriculture, and gorgeous landscapes made me think of the funky, native yeast-harboring ciders of France and Spain, an acquired taste for anyone accustomed to crushing Angry Orchard or the clean, delicate flavor of orchard-based cider. I wondered if Diane had ever experimented with any Old World cider techniques from Europe, where the big wooden fermenting vats have years of wild

yeasts all contributing to the funky flavors found in French and Spanish ciders. It's one of the characteristics that separates European cider from lighter, more delicate American varieties.

"I experimented with native yeasts as a home cider maker before I got my license," she said. "But I believe in a very clean ferment. When it came time to build our facility for making cider, I used stainless steel and concrete, and I wanted to be sure I could clean things with a pressure washer. So, the yeasts that could have come to me were more likely to come off the beards from the young men who were helping me press apples. However, if I were still making cider, it is something I would be experimenting with now."

Now that Diane, a four-time James Beard Nominee and someone the *Washington Post* has called "a prominent advocate and ambassador for the craft cider movement," has shuttered her cidery to slow down daily life and focus on the orchard itself, where are we to look for badass cider now? And who's getting these delicious apples of hers?

"I don't know if I could sell a hundred times the amount of apples we grow, but I could easily sell fifty times what we grow," she said, laughing. "There's a cidery in North Carolina called Molly Chomper and they do a lovely job and make delicious cider. In Virginia, we've got Courthouse Creek Cidery near Richmond, and they do a lot of experimentation and grow some of their own fruit. I really love their approach. Another one I'm excited about is Troddenvale Cider in Warm Springs, Virginia. They're using some of our fruit and I think there's a real promise to what they are doing over there, and they have a beautiful aesthetic. We can expect some great cider from them in the years to come."

There is indeed a bright future for orchard-based cider in Virginia and beyond. In early 2020, scientists at Cornell and in conjunction with Virginia Tech received a $500,000 grant to create a unified language for cider and to help foster its growth beyond the region. They even used some of Diane's fruit to study the complexities of the region's many different varieties. Diane is also working with the University of North Carolina to archive the work of Lee Calhoun, author of the Southern cider bible *Old Southern Apples*, an encyclopedic guide to all the hundreds of different apple varieties grown in the region for centuries. She'll also be writing a book of her own, telling the stories behind those different varieties. In the meantime, enjoy these cider-based cocktails. The ability to lengthen any large-format drink with cider, in lieu of champagne or, god help us, water, is a great party trick to keep in your back pocket. Good cider brightens any occasion, whether it's s'mores with the neighbors or that long-awaited family gathering. Here are some cider cocktails to enjoy in autumn, or any season.

Cider Spritz

4 oz. dry sparkling cider (like Brightwood Cider, Nashville)

1 oz. Salers apéritif (gentian liqueur)

2 marigold blossoms, if in season

1 oz. soda, Topo Chico

Garnish: thyme sprig or other aromatic herb

In a large wine glass filled ¾ of the way with ice, add the cider and Salers and briefly stir to incorporate. Add the marigold blossoms and stir to release the honeyed aroma. Top with the ounce of soda and garnish with the aromatic sprig.

The Cider Cocktail

2 dashes aromatic bitters

½ teaspoon maple syrup

Garnish: lemon twist

5 oz. dry sparkling cider

In a coupe or flute glass, add the bitters, maple syrup, and lemon twist, expressing the oils around the glass. Add the cider, and lightly stir ingredients to combine.

Apples to Apples

1 oz. Laird's Apple Brandy

½ oz. Lillet or Cocchi Americano

1 dash citrus bitters

3-4 oz. dry sparkling cider

Garnish: rosemary; thyme; apple slice

In a Collins or rocks glass, fill ¾ full with ice and add the brandy, Lillet or Cocchi, and bitters, and stir to mix ingredients. Add the cider, and stir a little more to incorporate everything. Garnish with rosemary, thyme, or an apple slice.

Apples and Oranges

1 oz. Laird's Apple Brandy

¼ oz. Cointreau or other orange liqueur (Grand Marnier would be a bold choice)

1 dash aromatic bitters

3-4 oz. dry sparkling cider

Garnish: orange twist; rosemary; thyme; apple slice

In a Collins or rocks glass, fill ¾ full with ice and add the brandy, Cointreau, and bitters, stirring to mix ingredients. Add the cider, stirring to incorporate everything. Garnish with an orange twist and rosemary, thyme, or an apple slice.

MERRY BREW, THE ULTIMATE AUTUMN CIDER PUNCH

When it came time for Chef Sean Brock to unveil the location for his new flagship restaurant in Nashville, Audrey, named after his grandma (who taught him how to grow and cook food), he had very specific instructions for me: "We're going to build a big fire in the middle of this construction site, right where the best table in the house is going to be, and we're going to cook a big batch of cider over it. Here, check this out," he said as he handed me *Foxfire: Appalachian Cookery*. He had it open to a section about warm beverages, and the first one that caught my eye was the aptly named "Merry Brew," a concoction of juiced or pressed apples, spices, a little citrus, and—if you really wanna turn up the party—some booze. Or did I just assume it said this, and add the booze on my own? I can't remember, as this was a pre-pandemic soiree all the way back in November of 2019, when a mask was for Halloween and social distancing just meant that you stayed home. This recipe is an adaptation from the Firefox book's version, but you can mix and match different apple varieties, and experiment with different spirits and elixirs to make your own Merry Brew.

Very Merry Brew

½ cup firmly packed brown sugar

3 sticks of cinnamon

1 tablespoon whole cloves

½ teaspoon allspice

1 teaspoon nutmeg

4 sprigs rosemary

4 sprigs thyme

5 slices of orange

2 quarts apple juice

Garnish: cinnamon stick; slice of orange or lemon; some rosemary

Combine ingredients in a non-reactive pot, bring to a simmer, and cook for 20 to 30 minutes. Serve in pre-warmed mugs, adding to each mug:

1¼ oz. apple brandy

¾ oz. Madeira (Broadbent Rainwater Madeira would be a great choice)

Garnish with a cinnamon stick, slice of orange or lemon, and some rosemary.

SOME FAVORITE LIQUID GOLD APPLE BRANDY CLASSICS

Jack Rose (classic)

2 oz. Laird's Apple Brandy

.¾ oz. lemon/lime (both juices split)

.¾ oz. grenadine (grenadine recipe on page 56)

1 dash aromatic bitters

Garnish: apple slice or cherry

Shake brandy, lemon/lime juice, grenadine, and bitters and strain into a coupe. Garnish with apple slice or cherry.

Grenadine recipe

2 cups pomegranate juice

2 tablespoons pomegranate molasses (available at ethnic food stores)

2 cups sugar

4 drops orange flower water

4 drops rose water

Combine pomegranate juice, molasses, and sugar and stir over low heat. Bring up to a medium simmer slowly for 10 minutes. Set aside to cool. Once cool, add the flower waters.

Jack Rose Jello Shot

3 oz. Laird's Apple Brandy

2 oz. lemon/lime juice

1 oz. grenadine

¼ cup cold water

2½ teaspoons (1 packet) unflavored gelatin

1 cup boiling water

Garnish: pomegranate seeds; small mint leaf

Combine the apple brandy, lemon/lime juice, and grenadine in a bowl and refrigerate until chilled. Add the gelatin cold water and let sit for four minutes. Add the boiling water and stir the mixture until the gelatin is dissolved. Pour the mixture into any mold you'd like to use—or a sheet pan—and refrigerate for 3 to 4 hours, or overnight. When ready to serve, garnish with pomegranate seeds and a small mint leaf.

Apple Brandy Manhattan

2 oz. Laird's Apple Brandy

¾ oz. sweet vermouth

1 teaspoon Nocino

1 dash aromatic bitters

Garnish: lemon twist or cherry

Stir brandy, vermouth, Nocino, and bitters in a mixing glass until well chilled. Serve up in a coupe (or any damn glass) and garnish with a lemon twist and/or a cherry.

Widow's Kiss

1½ oz. Calvados

¾ oz. yellow Chartreuse

¾ oz. Benedictine

2 dashes aromatic bitters

Garnish: a cherry

Stir Calvados, yellow Chartreuse, Benedictine, and bitters until well chilled, and serve up, or over one big rock; garnish with a cherry.

Apple Brandy Maple Old-Fashioned

1 thin lemon peel, as little pith as possible

Scant ¼ oz. maple syrup

2 dashes aromatic bitters

1 dash black walnut bitters (Fee's)

2 oz. Laird's Apple Brandy

Garnish: lemon peel

At the bottom of a mixing glass, very lightly muddle the thin lemon peel together with the maple syrup and bitters to create your old-fashioned "concentrate." Then add ice and the apple brandy, and stir until well chilled. Serve in an old-fashioned glass over a big ice cube or two, and garnish with a lemon peel, expressed and inserted into the glass.

NOCINO, SOMETHING TO MAKE FOR THANKSGIVING AND CHRISTMAS

If you happen to live in the Southeast, or any other region where the temperatures are a little warmer during the fall, you may be familiar with black walnut trees. They can be very messy and almost too aromatic to be around (when ripened, black walnuts' aroma can be so heady it can make you dizzy), but the inky, intense flavor living inside those walnuts is where the delicious after-dinner elixir known as Nocino comes from. I wrote about Nocino extensively in my book *Garden to Glass: Grow Your Drinks from the Ground Up*, and how you want to start gathering your walnuts (with gloves on!) in the summer months when they are unripened, green, and very intense. However, there are plenty of areas in the country where black walnuts ripen throughout the fall. As long as you're wearing thick gloves that you'll need to throw away afterward, turning ripe black walnuts into Nocino is a fun process that can easily turn into a yearly ritual when you realize how delicious it is. This is a process that you can start as late as September or early October, giving you a new tool in your drinking arsenal when Thanksgiving and Christmas roll around. Here is a fairly straightforward Nocino recipe, with cocktails to make with it once you've let time and alcohol do its magic.

Holiday Nocino

(for saving for Thanksgiving and Christmas, with added spice)

- 11 green walnuts, quartered
- 2 quarts grain alcohol
- 2 quarts water

4 quarts sugar

4 cardamom pods, cracked

4 cinnamon sticks, crushed with the back of a skillet on a towel on a firm countertop

3 star anise pods

2 tablespoons whole cloves

Zest of 2 lemons

Zest of 2 oranges

TO BEGIN: Place the walnuts in a 64-ounce Mason jar and fill the jar with grain alcohol, leaving an inch of space at the top. Let the walnuts infuse for 2 months in a cool, dry area at room temperature, shaking the jar once a week.

AFTER 2 MONTHS: Combine the water, sugar, cardamom, cinnamon sticks, star anise, and cloves in a large pot and bring to a medium simmer. Simmer for 20 minutes, then remove from the heat and place in the refrigerator to infuse overnight.

THE NEXT DAY: Strain the spiced syrup, and discard the whole spices. Add the lemon zest to the strained syrup. Wearing gloves, strain the walnut infusion and discard the walnuts. Add the spiced syrup and orange zest to the walnut infusion and set aside in a cool, dark place for 1 month to let the flavors meld and rest together.

WHEN READY TO DRINK: Strain out the lemon and orange zest and bottle the Nocino. It will keep for at least six months.

Picts and Me Rollin' 2

(sequel from Garden to Glass)

1 oz. Foursquare rum

1 oz. Laird's Apple Brandy

1 oz. Nocino (page 60)

¼ oz. sweet vermouth

1 dash Angostura bitters

Very tiny pinch Maldon sea salt

Garnish: lemon twist

Combine all the ingredients except the lemon in a mixing glass. Add plenty of ice, and stir until well chilled. Strain into a rocks glass over a few large ice cubes, and garnish with a lemon twist.

Nocino Manhattan

2 oz. rye whiskey

½ oz. sweet vermouth

½ oz. Nocino

2 dashes aromatic bitters

Garnish: orange twist; a cherry

Combine whiskey, vermouth, Nocino, and bitters in a mixing glass until well chilled, and serve up in a coupe or cocktail glass. Garnish with an orange twist and a cherry.

Nocino Dessert Drink

1½ oz. Nocino

1 oz. Nardini (or other sweet Amaro)

½ oz. sweet vermouth

Tiny pinch of salt

1 dash orange bitters

Garnish: star anise pod; orange peel

Stir Nocino, Nardini, vermouth, salt, and bitters until well chilled, and strain into a coupe glass. Garnish with a star anise pod and orange peel, expressed and discarded.

Night Train to Toronto

2 oz. rye whiskey

½ oz. Nocino

¼ oz. Fernet

¼ oz. Punt e Mes

1 teaspoon maple syrup

1 tiny pinch salt

Garnish: lemon twist

Stir whiskey, Nocino, Fernet, Pent e Mes, maple syrup, and salt until well chilled, and serve over a big ice cube in an old-fashioned glass. Garnish with a lemon twist.

Hot Buttered Cider

5 oz. Very Merry Brew (page 54), or other hot cider

2 oz. European-style butter

1¼ oz. aged dark rum (El Dorado 8 year, Appleton Estate, or Foursquare)

1 dash aromatic bitters

Garnish: 1 sprig thyme; dehydrated apple

Add the butter to the cup of hot cider, and stir to incorporate. Add the rum and bitters, and stir some more. Garnish with the sprig of thyme and a dehydrated apple.

Booze News APPLES

THE BEE AND THE ORCHARD

Orchardists all across the United States rent bees to help pollinate their crops. Cider farmers also pay hefty fees every year to combat the challenges of pesticidal detriment and increasing variants in the environment. In the meantime, bee farmers face their own challenges in increased demand and facilitation of transport. They are also very vulnerable to the same threats faced by sole-proprietor agriculturalists, as the proliferation of pesticides has shown detrimental to hive populations as well. What can a lone gardener do to help this situation? Don't use pesticides, and try to grow things like your ancient ancestors did: using cover crops to replenish the soil's nutrients, compost to add organic matter to the soil, and organic methods for pest prevention like Neem oil and Spinosad.

THE CIDER-APPLE PURGE

Although cider-apple varieties were prominent in the eastern United States in the nineteenth century, especially in Ohio, Michigan, Pennsylvania, and the Virginias, the growth into the West in the early twentieth century was held up by the passage of the Eighteenth Amendment and later the Volstead Act, prohibiting the production of alcohol in the United States and enforcing it amongst the states. High-volume orchards struggled overnight, and with little use for cider apples, the population shifted to sweeter, more edible varieties of apples. Many cideries burned old orchards to replant with a more immediately affordable crop. A resurgence of this colonial craft is under way all over the country, as old varieties are now being grafted and grown in many of their ancestors' soils.

A NEW APPLE VARIETY: RED DRAGON?

American as apple pie? Maybe, but it appears that China grows the most apples in the world, and will for a very long time. The United States produces its fair share, but only about a ninth of the tonnage that the Red Dragon generates. If you combined the number of apples the USA, Poland, and Turkey churn out (the 2nd, 3rd, and 4th worldwide producers, respectively), China would produce 3.5 times that amount.

WE PREFER PEARS TO BE IN A BOTTLE OF BOOZE

Pears are one of those fruits that immediately take me back to my childhood. The unmistakable aroma of ripened pear puts me back at the kitchen table as my mom encourages a fresh fruit accompaniment to my peanut butter and jelly. While I don't eat many pears anymore—we're more of an apple-a-day family—I do love the various pear spirits and liqueurs available to us today. And since pears tend to look brown-spotted and dented when they're ripe, they are perfect ingredients for homemade cordials and elixirs. You can also dehydrate pear slices for functional garnishes that are eye-catching (the dehydration process turns a pear slice into a textural little sculpture, see picture) and equally delicious.

The first time I saw Clear Creek Distillery's "Pear in a Bottle" brandy, I had to have it, based on looks alone. Here was a golden-hued, luscious spirit mingling with a whole pear encased in a long, gorgeous bottle. I bought some for the bar and began mixing a few cocktails with it and serving it as an after-dinner digestif. Customers would ask, "How do they get the pear in there?" Magic, I would say—but eventually I had to find out for myself. It turns out that this tradition goes back three hundred years to the Alsace region of France—known for producing delicious wines such as Riesling, Gewürztraminer, and a lovely sparkling wine called Crémant d'Alsace (all of which you can use at Thanksgiving). In the springtime, orchardists and staff traverse the pear orchards, delicately placing glass bottles in the trees, sliding immature pears into them, and tying the bottles against sturdy branches. The pear stays in the bottle as it matures throughout the summer months, then is cleaned along with the bottle and drenched in pear brandy from the previous harvest as the bottle is filled and capped.

Clear Creek Distillery is a big part of bringing back fruit-brandy production in the United States, a spirits category that flourished throughout the 1800s. We can also thank St. George Spirits out of California, who began distilling fruit brandies in the 1980s and have gone on to

produce singular expressions of everything from coffee liqueur to Rhum agricole and amazing gins (St. George Terroir is unlike any other gin; we cover it on page 329). While St. George makes a delicious pear brandy, their Spiced Pear Liqueur is a versatile standout in all manner of orchard-based autumnal cocktails. The French call pear brandy *eau de vie de poire,* or "pear water of life." I'm a believer. Here's a pear punch idea bringing together various flavors from the orchard.

Orchard Punch

Serves 4

4 oz. pear (in a bottle or not, whatever you can find) brandy

2 oz. apple brandy

2 oz. lemon juice

4 oz. Martinelli's apple juice

1½ oz. St. George Spiced Pear Liqueur

2 dashes aromatic bitters

½ oz. agave nectar

1 bottle apple or pear cider

Garnish: dehydrated pear slices and thyme

Place all ingredients, except for the cider and garnish, in a punch bowl and stir to combine. When it's time to serve, add ice and pour in the bottle of cider. Stir and garnish.

Dehydrated Pear Slices

8 pears, ripened and sliced to even thickness

Bowl of cold water

1 lemon, juiced

Dehydrator or oven

Wash the pears, lightly pat them dry, and remove the stems. Slice pears as evenly as possible in order to get a uniform shape. Squeeze the juice from one lemon into the bowl of cold water. Dip each slice of pear into the lemon water and blot dry with a paper towel before placing on the dehydrator tray or cookie sheet (if using the oven). This will help keep the pears from browning too much. Leave space

between the pear slices so plenty of air can circulate around them as they dehydrate. Most dehydrators recommend a temperature of 136°F to dehydrate fruit. If using an oven, try 150°F or the lowest possible setting on the oven. If stacking trays in a dehydrator, check to see if some trays are cooking faster than others, and move the trays around as needed during the process. Dehydrating pears in a dehydrator can take as long as 20 to 24 hours, while an oven set at 150°F can take between 6 and 9 hours. If you need the pears to dry out quickly, before the guests arrive, try dehydrating them in the oven at 225°F for 2 hours. Store the dehydrated pears in a container with a lid, away from sunlight. The pears will keep for 6 to 8 months.

Here are some other pear cocktails to enjoy in autumn.

Pear Ginger Collins

1½ oz. pear brandy

¼ oz. St. George Spiced Pear Liqueur

½ oz. lemon juice

1 dash aromatic bitters

Ginger beer to top (Blenheim)

Garnish: sage; slice of dehydrated pear

Combine the brandy, liqueur, lemon juice, and bitters in a Collins glass over ice, and briskly stir to incorporate. Top with ginger beer or ginger soda, and garnish with sage and a slice of dehydrated pear.

Pear in a Bottle Brandy Cosmo

1½ oz. pear brandy

¾ oz. lemon juice

½ oz. Grenadine

½ oz. dry Curaçao

1 barspoon simple syrup

1 dash Peychaud's bitters

Garnish: lemon wheel; parsley leaf

Shake ingredients until cold, and strain into a martini glass. Garnish with a floating lemon wheel and a leaf of parsley.

PEAR
GINGER
COLLINS
p. 73

Pear Brandy Prosecco Cocktail

1 oz. pear brandy

¼ oz. Amaro Nonino

1 dash aromatic bitters

4 oz. Prosecco

Garnish: orange twist

Stir the pear brandy, Amaro Nonino, and bitters together over ice until chilled. Strain into a Champagne flute or cocktail glass and top with the Prosecco. Garnish with an orange twist.

Calvados Pear Martinez

1½ oz. Calvados

¼ oz. St. George Spiced Pearl Liqueur

¾ oz. sweet vermouth

1 dash Boker's (or aromatic bitters)

Garnish: pear slice; lemon twist

Stir Calvados, liqueur, vermouth, and bitters until well chilled, and serve up in a coupe. Garnish with a pear slice and a lemon twist.

Booze News **PEARS**

PEARS AND PIGEONS, A LOVE STORY

My spirit animal, if I had to pick one—and since I'm a bartender and we get asked those kinds of questions, I do—would have to be the elephant. The marula tree in South Africa, related to mangoes, has long thrived as a source of food (and a good buzz) for elephants, due to their consumption of these fruits as they ferment. Often discounted, elephants live in an incredibly competitive environment, and the marula is considered the crème de la crème to many foragers in the area. Why would the fruit be allowed to ferment before being consumed by any number of hungry, hairy quadrupeds?

A lot of the math doesn't add up, though many scientists have compared the amount of alcohol by volume through consumption by African and Asian pachyderms to the same weight distribution of humans. It turns out that elephants lack a unique gene that facilitates ethanol breakdown. This gene is prevalent in many primates, with humans being the most efficient. The gene, ADH7, produces an enzyme called Alcohol Dehydrogenase, facilitating the flush of alcohol from the bloodstream. Other animals missing this gene are deer, horses, cows, and dogs. Be careful beering your pups, my friends. We don't recommend it.

Another animal possibly lacking the ADH7 gene is no one's spirit animal: pigeons! In the Marino suburb of Dublin, Ireland, citizens are put on alert as the overplanted, lush, productive pear harvest in early autumn leads to a pigeon-health nightmare. Over the years, the local pigeons have been documented to overconsume the fruit, appearing slightly intoxicated while gorging on slightly fermented pears that lie on the ground. There are numerous sources documenting the birds swaying, walking in circles, and even passed out with joints in their mouth. A good Samaritan once took one to a veterinarian, though thankfully they did *not* take it to brunch.

LOTS TO UNPACK WITH PEAR PACKAGING

Pears have long been packed in tissue paper as they make their long journey from the orchard to the supermarket. The reasons for this are many: pears have thin skin and can collide and bruise during transit; they are vulnerable to scald due to oxidation; and they are quite susceptible to fungal pathogens and mold, which can spread quickly when pears are packed together in a box. Initially coated in a food-grade oil in the early twentieth century, pears would soon be wrapped in paper that contained a Monsanto-created pesticide called ethoxyquin, as well as copper. Ethoxyquin is banned in the EU and Australia. The best way to avoid coming into contact with this pesticide is to buy organic pears. You can also aid in the quest for sustainability by purchasing imperfect pears (with brown spots or blotches), which are usually thrown out. This is especially true for those using pears to cook with, or for turning into jams and jellies.

THE OLDEST FRUIT TREE IN THE UNITED STATES

Behind a nondescript brick building at the bottom of a hill in an office park in Danvers, Massachusetts, sits the oldest cultivated fruit tree in the United States. This pear tree, planted by John Endecott at his estate in what most botanists agree was somewhere between 1630 and 1649, has withstood nearly four centuries of calamity, including four hurricanes between the years of 1804 and 1934. You'd expect the tree to look mightier and more gargantuan than it does. I hate to say it, but it looks like any old tree, certainly less impressive than many of the pear trees in my neighborhood in Nashville. There's a good reason, however. According to *Gastro Obscura*, in July 1964 vandals cut off the tree's branches and hacked away at its trunk. This should be the national symbol of "We can't have nice things." Regardless, the tree came back strong and is still bearing fruit as of this writing. Reviews and reports of how the fruit tastes go back hundreds of years and can be summed up in one word: tough.

Pumpkins,
Zombies,
and
Agavember

THREE

Persimmon, Pawpaw, and Pumpkin Spice

When English and Dutch settlers came to the New World, they were surprised to find an array of exotic fruit, especially in the Northeast and the South.

Wild berries of many different varieties, grapes, plums, the banana-like pawpaw, and a mysterious fruit that seemed nearly inedible at first: the persimmon. If you've ever tried to bite into a bright orange, firm, unripe persimmon, with its stem laid atop like green giftwrap, you probably have an idea of what these early settlers were tasting. Eating an unripe persimmon is like biting into a racquetball that's been left out in the rain. However—of course, it took the natives teaching them the mysterious ways of the persimmon—if you let this fruit ripen as much as possible on the tree (before the birds and raccoons get to them) pick it, and let it ripen some more to the point that it's almost mush, you suddenly have an incredibly diverse, complex, and delicious fruit on your hands. And it *will stick to your hands.* With a flavor ranging from mango pudding to pumpkin puree with the added spice, persimmons can be used for breads (a traditional native preparation), soups, desserts, pies, and, for our purposes, cordials. Along with pawpaw (more on page 108) and pumpkin (page 95), persimmon is a perfect ingredient for fall imbibing. And it offers the ultimate lesson in waiting until an ingredient is just right.

As fruit ripens, the starches begin to break down, which corresponds with a rise in sugar levels and an overall breakdown in structure. This is the key to working with persimmon, pumpkin, and pawpaw. Once the fruit (or gourd, in the case of the pumpkin) is fully ripened, you'll be able to smell all the possibilities that lie within its cell walls. The reason pumpkin spice is in our lives is because the fully ripened flavor of pumpkin already hints at all those beautiful spices. I think you'll find that persimmon does too, and is a beautiful ingredient to rediscover in a season when fully ripened fruits can be hard to come by.

Persimmon Spice Demerara

2 pints of fully ripened (soft and mushy) persimmons

2 cups turbinado sugar

1 cup water

DRY SPICES:

1 tablespoon cinnamon

1 tablespoon clove

1 tablespoon allspice

1 teaspoon freshly grated nutmeg (use a Microplane)

1 teaspoon star anise

Combine the dry spices in a mortar and pestle, and crush until broken up. In a saucepan, combine the crushed spices and ripened persimmons along with the sugar and water and bring to a boil, mashing the persimmons with the back of a wooden spoon in the process. Immediately turn down the heat to a low simmer and cook, covered, for 15 minutes. Remove from heat and let cool. Allow the cordial to infuse overnight, or 2 days for a bolder flavor. Strain through a fine sieve. Stored in the refrigerator, the cordial will keep for 3 weeks. Add an ounce of vodka to keep the cordial fresh for 6 to 8 weeks.

Persimmon Spice Old-Fashioned

---

2 oz. rye whiskey (bourbon is fine too!)

¼ oz. persimmon demerara

2 dashes aromatic bitters

3 drops allspice dram

Garnish: orange peel; sprig of thyme

Stir whiskey, demerara, bitters, and allspice until well chilled, and strain into an old-fashioned glass with a large ice cube or two. Garnish with an orange peel and a sprig of thyme.

Persimmon Whiskey Punch

Serves 6–8

4 oz. bourbon or rye

2 oz. sweet vermouth

2 oz. lemon juice

4 oz. Martinelli's apple juice, or juiced local apples

1½ oz. persimmon demerara

6 dashes aromatic bitters

Pinch of salt

1 bottle sparkling wine or sparkling cider

Garnish: dehydrated persimmon slices (see page 88); thyme

Place bourbon, vermouth, lemon juice, apple juice, demerara, bitters, and salt in a punch bowl, and stir to combine. When it's time to serve, add ice and pour in the bottle of sparkling wine or cider. Stir and garnish.

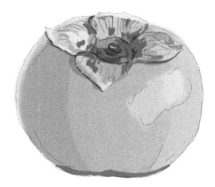

Dehydrated
Persimmon Slices

8 persimmons, ripened but not too mushy, and sliced to even thickness

Bowl of cold water

1 lemon, juiced

Dehydrator or oven

Wash the persimmons, lightly pat them dry, and remove the top stem portion. Slice the persimmons as evenly as possible in order to get a uniform shape. Squeeze the juice from one lemon into the bowl of cold water. Dip each slice of persimmon into the lemon water and blot dry with a paper towel before placing on the dehydrator tray or cookie sheet (if using the oven). This will help keep the persimmons from becoming too dark in color. Leave space between slices so plenty of air can circulate as they dehydrate.

Most dehydrators recommend a temperature of 136°F to dehydrate fruit. If using an oven, try 150°F or the lowest possible setting on the oven. If stacking trays in a dehydrator, check to see if one tray is cooking faster than others, and move the trays around as needed during the process. Dehydrating persimmons in a dehydrator can take as many as 10 to 24 hours, while an oven set at 150°F can take between 6 and 9 hours. If you need them to dry out faster, try dehydrating the persimmons in the oven at 225°F for 2 hours. Store the slices in a container with a lid, away from sunlight. They will keep for 6 to 8 months.

Persimmon Manhattan

2 oz. rye whiskey

½ oz. sweet vermouth (something with a nice spiced characteristic to blend with the persimmon flavor, like Cocchi Torino of Italy)

¼ oz. persimmon demerara

3 dashes aromatic bitters

Garnish: dehydrated persimmon slices; thyme

Stir whiskey, vermouth, demerara, and bitters until well chilled, let sit for 5 minutes, then strain into a chilled coupe or a rocks glass with one big ice cube and garnish with an orange twist and a cherry.

Persimmon Manhattan

Batched for 6

12 oz. rye whiskey

6 oz. sweet vermouth (something with a nice spiced characteristic to blend with the persimmon flavor, like Cocchi Torino of Italy)

2 oz. persimmon demerara

6 oz. water

12 dashes aromatic bitters

Garnish: dehydrated persimmon slices; thyme

Stir whiskey, vermouth, demerara, water, and bitters in a large pitcher or punch bowl without ice until well mixed. Cover and refrigerate. To serve, pour into rocks glasses and garnish with orange peel and thyme. For a celebratory flourish, garnish with dehydrated persimmon slices and thyme.

Persimmon Whiskey Sour

2 oz. bourbon or rye whiskey

¾ oz. fresh lemon juice

½ oz. persimmon demerara

White of one egg (save the yolk to fold into your favorite pasta dish for dinner)

1 dash aromatic bitters

1 dash citrus bitters

Garnish: half lemon wheel

In a shaker, combine bourbon, lemon juice, demerara, egg white, and bitters and shake for 30 seconds or so to incorporate the egg. Then add one or two big ice cubes and shake vigorously while dancing in your kitchen. When you notice the ice cubes have nearly dissolved, strain the drink into a coupe or rocks glass. Garnish with a half lemon wheel and a sprinkling of bitters on top of the egg white foam.

Booze News PERSIMMONS

PERSIMMON TAKES ON A HEALTH FOOD LEGEND

In a report from sciencedaily.com, the American Chemical Society has determined that a persimmon a day can do more for your heart health than an apple a day. A head-to-head comparison of the two fall fruits by an international group of researchers found that persimmons contain significantly higher concentrations of dietary fiber, minerals, and phenolic compounds, which are all instrumental in fighting heart disease and strokes. This was the first side-by-side study between the two fruits. In a previous study, persimmons were found to increase lipid metabolism in rats. The article notes that while persimmon trees grow wild in the United States, most of the persimmons grown for consumption in the US come from Japan.

ROTTEN OR RIPE?

Thomas Harriot, an Oxford-educated nautical engineer, said the whitest thing, which also happens to be the first reference to persimmons in Western culture in the Americas. Introduced to the fruit for the first time, he made note that it was eaten by Native Americans when "rotten" in his 1588 writing *A Brief and True Report of the New Found Land of Virginia*. In 1612, John Smith would correct Harriot's verbiage, requiring the ingestion of persimmon to be "ripe" before consumption.

Persimmon was plentiful as any abundant food from the forest, and the growing number of hunters and trappers took notice. Finding groves of persimmon meant finding deer and bear meat, hides, and plenty of this perfectly rotten/ripe fruit. Although the persimmon is not acknowledged by many as a fruit that was widely accepted by the colonists (they were rapidly adapting to corn cultivation in these times), the apple and pear were planted often in the New World. Though they were not indigenous, they thrived in a way not possible in England.

PUMPKIN / NOT SOBER OCTOBER

#OCTOBERNOTSOBER
#NOTSOBEROCTOBER

When it came time to finally unveil the private dining space at Husk in Nashville, dubbed The Stables—as it once had housed the horses of the original inhabitants of the house on Rutledge Hill, over 130 years ago— the first thing we did was to invite the media, along with food bloggers and social-media thirst trappers, to show off the new space, complete with its own patio with views of the garden. The pressure was on for me

to create an eye-catching punch for the guests that would accomplish three things: to be subtly strong enough to give people a nice little buzz to enjoy with their snacks; to break the ice of social awkwardness often inevitable at these events; and to create an eye-catching, small photo op (who's thirsty now? you ask) in its own right. For events like these, and holiday parties and backyard barbecues alike, I love using an actual ingredient—like watermelon or pumpkin—in the punch *and to serve the punch out of.* So, since it was pumpkin season, I made a pumpkin spice cordial (see page 98), hollowed out a huge, beautiful pumpkin from the market, and made an eye-catching ice cube by dropping a few leaves of ornamental purple kale and some bright red mums into a Tupperware container and placing it in the freezer. If you're hosting family and/or friends this year, or just need an excuse to dress up a punchbowl because you haven't celebrated with people in a really long time, this punch is a great way to dress up the occasion, without changing from your jeans.

Punchkin (Punch in a Pumpkin)

Serves 10 to 14 guests

2 pints (4 cups) fall spiced or black tea (hot)

½ cup demerara sugar

½ cup honey

1 cup lemon juice (strained)

2 cups bourbon

2 cups aged rum (El Dorado 8 year would be a great choice here)

Garnish: fresh nutmeg; 3 sprigs thyme; 2 cinnamon sticks

Also: 1 large pumpkin (see below)

For the ice mold: 5 star anise pods (see below)

1 large freezer-proof bowl or Tupperware

PUMPKIN AND ICE MOLD: Hollow out the pumpkin the same as if you were preparing it to be carved, leaving a larger hole at the top since you'll be serving punch out of it. Scrape out as much of the pumpkin meat as you can for the cleanest presentation possible. Save all the pumpkin meat and seeds to make pumpkin cordial (see page 100). For the ice mold, take a large freezer-proof bowl (one that will allow you to slide the big ice cube into the pumpkin later) and fill it with water and the star anise pods and place in the freezer. With a spoon, gently try to separate the star anise pods around the bowl before it freezes, for a more even distribution.

THE PUNCH: While the freshly brewed tea is hot, add the sugar and honey, stirring to dissolve. Let the tea syrup cool in the refrigerator. Once cooled, add to the hollowed-out pumpkin: tea syrup, the fresh lemon juice, bourbon, and rum. Stir to combine. Garnish with plenty of freshly grated nutmeg, 3 sprigs of thyme, and the ice mold. Place the cinnamon sticks on top of the mold so you've got that cool "some spices are frozen while some are not" vibe. Take a picture now, because I'm sure it won't be that beautiful for too long, once the guests start diving in. If the punch tastes too strong for you and your guests, add water, 2 ounces at a time.

Pumpkin Spice Cordial

2 cups canned pumpkin (pumpkin puree) or pumpkin meat from the "punch pumpkin"

2 cups turbinado sugar

1¾ cups water

4 oz. Italian (or any chocolatey) vermouth

Zest of one orange

DRY SPICES:

3 tablespoons cinnamon

2 tablespoons clove

2 tablespoons allspice

1 tablespoon freshly grated nutmeg (use a Microplane)

2 teaspoons cinnamon/cassia flower buds

1 tablespoon star anise

1 teaspoon Chinese five spice

1 teaspoon cardamom

Combine the dry spices in a mortar and pestle and crush them together with a firm but steady hand. Toast the dry spices together in a cast-iron skillet over medium-low heat, being careful not to burn or deeply color the spices. Toast them just enough to wake up the aroma and give life to them.

In a saucepan, combine the pumpkin puree, sugar, water, and vermouth, and bring to a gentle boil, stirring to dissolve the sugar. Add the toasted spices to the cordial as it cooks, and stir them into the mixture. Turn the heat down to a low simmer for 20 minutes, and set aside, covered.

Let the syrup sit, covered and cooling, for 4 to 6 hours, then put it in the refrigerator. Strain the next day (or longer for deeper flavor; taste and test).

FINISHING: When you're ready to strain the cordial, begin by adding the zest of one orange into the cordial, to freshen it up and add some lively aromatics. Let the zest sit in the cordial for one hour. Then strain everything through a fine sieve, bottle, label, and store in the refrigerator. It will keep for a month, but will stay fresh for up to 3 months if you add an ounce of vodka or whiskey.

Pumpkin Cordial (hold the spice):

Putting the focus on bringing out the actual pumpkin flavor

1 pie pumpkin (the small ones that are the size of a mini-basketball) from as local a source as possible

1 bunch of fresh thyme (8 to 10 sprigs)

2 sprigs of rosemary

6 to 8 sage leaves

1 bay leaf

Freshly cracked black pepper

1 large pinch of salt

FOR THE SYRUP:

4 cups turbinado sugar

2 cups water

Slice open the top of the pumpkin and create some space for the aromatics to sit inside. Place the thyme, rosemary, sage, and bay inside the pumpkin, and also crack a few turns of black pepper. Sprinkle salt over the aromatics like you're seasoning a fish, and put the top back on the pumpkin. Roast the pumpkin at 400°F for one hour. After roasting, allow the pumpkin to cool before handling it. As it cools, prepare the syrup. Bring the 4 cups of sugar and 2 cups of water to a boil and immediately turn down the heat to a low simmer. Begin scraping out the pumpkin meat from the roasted pumpkin, along with the aromatics. Add the pumpkin and the aromatics to the syrup as it simmers, letting the pumpkin cook in the syrup for 15 minutes. Infuse the syrup overnight in the refrigerator and strain through a fine sieve the next day. For a bolder flavor, let the pumpkin infuse in the syrup for 2 to 3 days. Bottled and kept in the refrigerator, the cordial will keep for 3 weeks.

Pumpkin-infused Vermouth

1 cup pumpkin puree

1 (750-ml) bottle of sweet vermouth (preferably something bold like Carpano Antica, Punt e Mes, or Cocchi Torino)

Dash of powdered cinnamon

Dash of freshly ground nutmeg

1 teaspoon allspice dram

Combine ingredients in a bowl, and mix to combine. Bottle and keep in the refrigerator. For best taste, use within one month.

Pumpkin Spice Espresso Martini

1 oz. vodka

¾ oz. coffee liqueur (St. George New Orleans Coffee Liqueur)

1 oz. cold brew

¾ oz. Pumpkin Spice Cordial

1 dash aromatic bitters

Garnish: coffee or espresso beans

Shake vodka, liqueur, cold brew, cordial, and bitters and strain into a cocktail glass. Garnish with 3 coffee or espresso beans.

Pumpkin Manhattan

2 oz. bourbon or rye whiskey

¾ oz. pumpkin vermouth (recipe on page 102)

1 barspoon spiced or unspiced pumpkin cordial

2 dashes aromatic bitters

Garnish: orange peel; a cherry

Stir ingredients until well chilled and serve up. Garnish with an orange twist and a cherry.

Pumpkin Manhattan

Batched for 6

12 oz. rye whiskey

6 oz. pumpkin-infused sweet vermouth (recipe on page 102)

1 oz. Pumpkin Spice Cordial

6 oz. water

12 dashes aromatic bitters

Garnish: orange peel; cherry; thyme

Stir ingredients in a large pitcher or punch bowl without ice until well mixed. Cover and refrigerate. To serve, pour into rocks glasses and garnish with orange twist and a cherry, or thyme sprig. For a celebratory flourish, top with sparkling wine or cider.

Pumpkin Boulevardier

1½ oz. bourbon

1 oz. Campari

1 oz. pumpkin-infused vermouth (recipe on page 102)

Tiny pinch salt

Garnish: orange peel; orange slice

Stir bourbon, Campari, vermouth, and salt until well chilled, and serve over a few big ice cubes in an old-fashioned glass. Garnish with an orange peel and an orange slice.

Booze News **PUMPKIN**

PLANT A PUMPKIN, SAVE THE WORLD

Dichlorodiphenyltrichloroethane (DDT) was the raging pesticide of the Boomer generation. It was sprayed along roadsides and fields, causing dire consequences to wildlife everywhere. As many pests developed a resistance and resurgence, birds like the bald eagle would suffer catastrophic reproductive implications. Toxic to most animals, DDT eventually wedged itself into nature's food chain.

Banned in the United States in 1972, there is still no definitive study on its long-term effects on humans, while the average contamination rate is around ten times less per person than it was at the time of the ban. Still used, rarely, in the fight against malaria, the WHO has all but prohibited it elsewhere unless the benefits of not contracting malaria outweigh the perceived long-term detriment to the populace in hard-stricken areas of Africa, Asia, and South America.

DDT is hydrophobic, meaning it is not water-soluble. It bonds with oils, and humans carry it in their fat cells. It easily bonds with organic oils in soils and chains itself to the ground, risking further detriment to animal life in the distant future.

Enter Ken Reimer of the Royal Military College of Canada and his colleagues, Alissa Lunny and Barbara Zeeb, experts in the technology of phytoremediation. They are developing a plant-based approach for cleaning ionic contaminants from soil damaged by years of DDT use. In a study of pumpkins, alfalfa, rye grain, fescue, and zucchini, it was pumpkin and zucchini—members of the Cucurbita Pepo family of plants—that outperformed others at removing DDT from contaminated soil. Scientists theorize that the species's vast root system, coupled with eventual above-ground mass, likely creates this soil-filtering result. Now go get your pumpkin seeds!

AMERICA: FIRST IN LATTÉS, FIFTH IN FARMING

Although pumpkins are indigenous to the Americas, the pepita, or pumpkin seed, has spread around the globe. In fact, China produces the most pumpkins on the planet, passing India, who led for decades. Russia and Ukraine come in tied for third and fourth place. The United States jogs in at fifth. But damn, do we make a good latté.

PAWPAW: BIG FLAVORS WITH THE WILDEST FRUIT IN NORTH AMERICA

Pawpaws, the tropical-tasting, bulbous, mysterious fruit found in forests all over the southeastern and midwestern United States, have had a long history, from cultivation by Native Americans to appreciation by hungry settlers, from a delicacy of the New World to a neglected forest-dweller. Now, pawpaws are ready for their moment of rediscovery. This is the same fruit that during the Great Depression was referred to as "poor man's bananas," and which George Washington devoured in desserts and Thomas Jefferson propagated all over his expansive garden at Monticello. The pawpaw's singularity can be summed up by the fact that it is the only temperate member of a family of tropical trees. It has been both exalted and mostly forgotten. Pet names include "Hillbilly Mango" and "Hipster's Banana," which would also be decent bluegrass band names. Technically the largest fruit native to North America, pawpaw's soft, custard-like texture tastes like a blend of mango, guava, and banana and arrives in late September/early October, a time when those summery, exotic flavors are hard to come by.

Even though they might be sitting up in a tree just waiting to be plucked near your house, pawpaws can be difficult to source during their short season. Luckily, there are a few reliable internet resources in the search for pawpaw glory: Owen Native Foods and Peterson Pawpaws both sell a variety of seeds, starter trees, frozen purees of pawpaw, and even salsas. To pluck your own pawpaw straight off the tree (assuming you live in the middle or southeast of the country), follow these simple foraging guidelines and consult the experts in the field (botanists, naturalists, park rangers, the internet) along the way:

+ Even in warm weather, wear protective clothing and boots in case you run into any poison ivy or other harmful pests. Carry some water while you're at it.

+ In humid climates, be mindful of mosquitoes and ticks. There are plenty of natural and organic bug-repellent options out there. We like Thistle Farms' and other essential-oil-based repellents.

+ Always cross-check whichever plant you're seeking out with any poisonous lookalikes. If you're ever in doubt of a plant or flower of any kind, definitely don't eat it. As for pawpaws, there are no poisonous lookalikes, and the large leaves on the tree are pretty distinct and recognizable.

+ For pawpaws, begin scouting for trees in August and try to notice any fruit-bearing trees with the signature banana-esque medallion of green and golden oblong fruit. Most trees fruit every other year, and sometimes finding a pawpaw tree doesn't necessarily mean finding the fruit—though you can make a note about that tree for next year.

+ Be gentle when harvesting pawpaw: the skin can be very soft and will bruise easily. Store with care, and let the fruit fully ripen before eating or cooking with it.

+ Be advised: According to scientist and avowed pawpaw enthusi-ast Neal Peterson, any fruit leather made with pawpaw has been shown to cause stomach discomfort, so don't get too weird out there, foodies.

Here are some techniques and recipes for getting the most out of your pawpaw drinking experience.

Pawpaw Frozen Daiquiri

Serves 2

4 oz. white or gold rum

2 oz. lime juice

1 oz. pawpaw cordial (see below)

1 oz. simple syrup

1 ripened pawpaw, fruit scooped out and seeds removed

1 dash cinnamon bitters (see page 116)

10 oz. crushed or cracked ice

Garnish: star anise pod; half lime wheels

Add rum, lime juice, simple syrup, pawpaw, bitters, and ice to a blender and blend at high speed for 10 seconds. Serve in coupe glasses, and garnish with a half wheel of lime and one star anise pod over the top.

Pawpaw Cordial

2 cups turbinado sugar

2 cups water

3 fully ripened pawpaws, fruit scooped out or diced

Pinch of salt

1 teaspoon grated cinnamon

Zest of 2 limes

4 oz. lime juice

Bring the sugar and water to a boil to dissolve the sugar, turn the heat down to a medium simmer, and add the pawpaw fruit. Add the salt and cinnamon and let the mixture simmer for 20 minutes. Remove from heat, add the lime zest, cover, and let the pawpaw infuse into the cordial on the countertop for 4 to 5 hours. Strain the mixture into a sealable container, add the lime juice, and store in the refrigerator. It will keep for at least a month.

Pawpaw Bitters

1 pint Mason jar

2 cinnamon sticks

1 tablespoon allspice berries

1 star anise pod

6 cloves

1 teaspoon gentian root

2 pawpaws, fruit scooped out and seeds removed

½ cup demerara sugar

½ cup water

12 oz. Wray and Nephew Overproof Rum

Crush the cinnamon, allspice, and star anise together in a mortar and pestle until broken up. Add them—along with the cloves, gentian, and pawpaws—to a pint Mason jar and top with the rum. Store in a cool place away from sunlight, and shake daily (or as much as you can) for 2 weeks. Taste after a few weeks and see how the flavors are melding. For a stronger flavor, keep the infusion going for another 2 weeks, once again shaking the mixture daily if possible. Once the infusion is to your liking, strain out the solids from the pint Mason jar and set the solids aside to use in the syrup.

In a saucepan, combine the sugar, water, and strained spices, and bring to a boil. Once boiling, lower heat immediately to a simmer for

20 minutes. Strain out the spices and let the syrup cool completely. Once cooled, add the bitters mixture, a tablespoon at a time, until you're happy with the taste. You want strong, fruity tropical notes from the pawpaw, mild spice, mild bitterness, and a little sweetness to make your bitters delicious and easy to work with. Bottled in a dark dropper bottle, these bitters will keep for at least a year.

Pawpaw Pureé

3 fully ripened pawpaws, fruit scooped out and seeds removed

½ cup sugar

½ cup water

Pre-heat the oven to 400°F. Place the pawpaws on a roasting pan and roast in the oven for 30 minutes or until lightly caramelized. Allow to cool slightly. Combine the roasted fruit, sugar, and water in a food processor and blend until smooth. Sealed and kept in the refrigerator, the puree will last for up to 4 days. To keep it fresher longer, keep it in the freezer in smaller containers and thaw when you need it.

Booze News **PAWPAW**

LEWIS AND CLARK GIVE THANKS FOR THE PAWPAW, 1806

According to History Net's informative article on pawpaws, Lewis and Clark's men escaped near starvation by eating pawpaws until they reached a settlement with provisions 150 miles down the river. A journal entry from September 18, 1806, notes that the men are "entirely out of provisions," though they "appear perfectly contented to tell us that they can live very well on the pawpaws." The fruit is loaded with vitamin C and antioxidants, and has the distinction of being the only fruit containing all the essential amino acids. The zebra swallowtail butterfly tends to agree, as it only lays eggs on the leaves of pawpaw trees.

CRAFT BEER AND PAWPAWS: A LOVE STORY

According to Owen Native Foods, growers and sellers of pawpaw fruit, the demand for pawpaws from craft breweries in Virginia outpaced the fresh-fruit retail market for the first time in 2020, and has been steadily increasing ever since. Some of the more notable beers nationwide to feature pawpaw include the Fonta Flora Carolina Custard from Morgantown, North Carolina, and the Urban Artifact Dilophosaurus Pawpaw from Cincinnati. One of the longest-running pawpaw beers, about to celebrate their tenth anniversary of brewing with America's native fruit, Jackie O's Pawpaw Wheat is made in Athens, Ohio, for the annual Ohio pawpaw festival in September. Seth Morton, Jackie O's head brewer, told *Beer and Brewing* magazine that he sources his pawpaws from Integration Acres in Athens County. "Thanks to them, we're able to purchase frozen pawpaw puree whenever we need it." Cheers to keepers of the pawpaw tropical flame.

FLAVORS TO FALL BACK ON

While pumpkins, persimmons, and pawpaws give us plenty of alliterative and delicious flavor combinations for autumn imbibing, it can also be fun to lean into the spice characteristics of the season to liven up everyday old-fashioneds, Manhattans, or your nightly cup of tea. What follows are cordial, bitters, and tea recipes suited for the season when it's still warm during the afternoon, though the night chill makes you think and drink differently than those endless summer nights. The cinnamon bitters can be used in place of Angostura bitters in almost any drink you make this time of year. And though none of us is really sure if chai tea is still cool or not, we do know it's delicious and pairs *really well* with whiskey and rum.

Thyme Cordial

2 cups water

2 cups sugar

1 large bunch thyme sprigs

3 or 4 sprigs of lemon thyme, if available

1 turn of cracked black pepper

Zest of 1 lemon

In a saucepan, combine the water, sugar, and thyme, and bring to a boil. Immediately reduce the heat to a medium simmer, and crack a few turns of black pepper into the cordial. Simmer for 30 minutes, covered. Remove from heat. Once cooled, add the lemon zest and transfer to the refrigerator. Let sit overnight, or a few days for a bolder flavor. Strain through a fine sieve, bottle, and refrigerate. It will keep for 6 weeks. Adding an ounce of vodka will increase shelf life by a few months.

Cinnamon Bitters

(Modern Angostura is missing its familiar cinnamon kick, and these can be used in tandem)

1 32-oz. Mason jar

12 oz. of cinnamon sticks, crushed and toasted (using a digital scale, you'll need a little less than a pound)

2 star anise pods

4 cloves

2 allspice berries (whole)

1 tablespoon gentian root (available from Mountain Rose Herbs and other online retailers)

Zest of 1 orange, dried (zest an orange and dry on a plate on your countertop overnight)

30 oz. 100-proof vodka

4 oz. rich demerara syrup (2 parts turbinado sugar to one part water, heated to dissolve the sugar)

Using the back of a cast-iron skillet on a firm countertop, crush the cinnamon sticks. Then add the star anise, cloves, and allspice and crush together with the cinnamon. Add the spices to a skillet over medium-low heat and toast lightly, taking care not to overcook or burn the spices. Transfer them to a plate to allow them to cool. Once cooled, add them to a 32-ounce Mason jar, along with the gentian, vodka, and dried orange zest, and let sit in a cool, dry place in your kitchen away from sunlight. As often as once a day (or a little less, if the day gets away from you), shake the mixture briskly to get as much extraction from your botanicals as possible. Taste the mixture every 3 or 4 days to see how the flavor increases. After 3 weeks, if you're happy with the extraction and intensity of the flavor, strain out the solids through cheesecloth and add the rich demerara syrup. The bitters will keep for at least a year.

Fall Spice Tea

2 pints (4 cups) water

1 tablespoon crushed cinnamon

1 tablespoon clove

1 teaspoon allspice

1 teaspoon freshly grated nutmeg (use a Microplane)

1 teaspoon cassia buds

3 star anise pods

½ teaspoon Chinese five spice

Crush spices in a mortar and pestle. Bring water to boil. Once boiling, turn down the heat a little, add the spices, and simmer for 20 minutes. Remove from heat and allow to cool. Steep for another hour, covered, then strain and refrigerate. Ideal for adding to punches, cordials, non-alcoholic drinks, and desserts.

Chai-infused Rye

1 32-oz. Mason jar

32 oz. rye (substitute bourbon or rum if you like!)

3 bags chai tea

Pour the rye—or any spirit of your choice—into the Mason jar and add the 3 bags of chai. Place the jar in a cool, dark place in the kitchen and shake every other day for a week. Take out the tea bags (no need to wring more flavor out of the tea by pressing on the bag; you run the risk of making it too astringent). Keep the chai-infused spirit in the Mason jar with the lid on, or pour it back into the bottle. The flavor will stay fresh for 3 months.

Make Your Own Chai Tea

2 cups Fall Spice Tea (see page 117)

2 cups milk (almond, oat, and coconut milk are great substitutions)

2 cups water

1 black tea bag

Sugar or honey, to taste

In a large pot, bring the fall spice tea, milk, and water to a medium simmer. Add the black tea bag, then turn down the heat to a low simmer for 5 minutes. Remove from heat, take out the tea bags, and pour into pre-warmed mugs. Sweeten the tea to taste (take note that traditional chai in India is sweetened by adding roughly a tablespoon of sugar per mug of tea). Honey is also a nice option to pair with the spices and milk as well.

Chai Rye Whiskey Punch

Serves 6–8

5 oz. Chai-Infused Rye (see page 117)

1 oz. sweet vermouth

1 oz. Amaro Averna (available at most well-stocked liquor stores)

2 oz. lemon juice

4 oz. Fall Spice Tea (see page 117)

1½ oz. thyme cordial (see page 115)

6 dashes cinnamon bitters (see page 116)

Pinch of salt

1 bottle sparkling wine

Garnish: dehydrated pear or persimmon slices; thyme

Place rye, vermouth, Amaro Averna, lemon juice, tea, cordial, bitters, and salt in a punch bowl and stir to combine. When it's time to serve, add ice and pour in the bottle of sparkling wine. Stir and garnish.

Chai Buttered Rum

(see more buttered drinks on page 195)

   1 tablespoon butter (cut in half to make two pats of butter)

   8 oz. chai tea (see page 118)

   1¼ oz. aged rum (try anything El Dorado or Hamilton makes)

   2 dashes cinnamon bitters (see page 116)

   1 dash apple cider vinegar

   Garnish: 1 small lemon wedge

Begin by tempering the mug you'll be drinking out of with hot water. Place a small bowl or plate on top of the mug to seal in the heat. After the mug is piping hot, take off the plate and discard the hot water. Add the butter, hot chai tea, rum, bitters, and apple cider vinegar and stir gently for 10 seconds. Squeeze a few drops of lemon juice over the top of the drink and garnish with the lemon wedge on the side of the mug. Forget about your troubles for a while.

FOUR

Halloween and Revealing the Zombie

When Don the Beachcomber, AKA Donn Beach—the godfather of tiki drinks—created his masterpiece "rum rhapsody," the Zombie, in 1934, it's unclear what his motivation was.

Advising guests to have no more than two (which later became one) during a visit to his tropical oasis at 1722 N. McCadden Place in Hollywood—the mecca of mythmaking—Donn Beach introduced the Zombie, the strongest drink to enter the canon of classic cocktails over the last 150 years. Due to the resurgence of tropical-themed bars and drinks over the last ten years, the drink—in true undead fashion—is here to stay. But was it, as legend has it, concocted as the ultimate hangover remedy? That's like saying I'm going to make you a double cheeseburger on a butter-brushed bun to help with your heart problem. Was it a sly middle finger to all the guests who, upon sampling the first fresh tropical libations that glide down the gullet like a Polynesian waterfall, wondered if there was even any alcohol in them? That's definitely something a bartender would do, but still doubtful. I've come to believe—and Jeff "Beachbum" Berry's thoughtful research in the book *Surfin' Safari* has greatly contributed to what we know about the Zombie, including the lost recipes—that Don the Beachcomber was using broad, ambitious brush-strokes to create a drink that defined his idea of the tropical restaurant/bar, would be impossible to recreate, and would prove unforgettable to all who experienced it. Though he claimed to have gone through gallons of rum to come up with just the right blend, he undoubtedly succeeded on all fronts. The Zombie was an instant classic and was seen as a rite of passage to locals and tourists alike in late-1930s Hollywood.

When it came time for me to create my own riff on the Zombie, it began as the ultimate "shift drink"—that all-important first drink you have when you get off work in the restaurant and bar world. This was a drink for professionals. It was not something I was making for guests at that point. But I learned quickly that once you say to a guest "This drink is too strong, it's got a ton of rum, and trust me, you don't want this concoction of tropical delight and dangerous firewater," it becomes *exactly what they want.* As I learned while testing out my version of the Zombie on coworkers at the time, people will really open up to you as a bartender if they drink a Zombie right in front of you. People began to confide in me in a way they never had, telling me things about their family, their childhood—it was quite the social experiment. I would say things like, "It's all right, we have bartender-client privilege, I won't say a thing to anybody about it." That's when the drink came to be known as "The Reveal," since most of the people who drank one would soon start revealing their secrets and telling me how they really felt about things. Initially my version of the Zombie was inspired by the Zombies of the 1940s and '50s, when pineapple juice and passion fruit became common modifiers to the original formula of three different rums, lime, grapefruit, cinnamon, falernum (page 127), absinthe, and grenadine. Later I would combine lemon and lime juice for a harmonious citrus kick. This was 2012, and tropical drinks weren't yet back in vogue with most customers. However, bartenders were well on their way to reviving the lost ingredients of tiki drinking culture, and many of these drinks were served not only by bartenders but between bartenders. And the Reveal would eventually have its day.

In 2017, with the tropical-drinks revival gaining steam, I embarked on a perilous journey with a few other entrepreneurs to open up our very own temple to the tiki gods, Chopper. Looking to avoid some of the cultural appropriation pitfalls and the overwrought kitsch of the early tiki bars, we looked to create our own universe with a world of robots that had gone undiscovered on a fictional deserted island in the South Pacific. Though it took over two years to complete—a sixteen-foot-tall robot replica hovering horizontally over the bar takes time—it opened to rave reviews and lines around the block. A few months in, the "drink of the summer of 2019 in Nashville" was prominently featured on the cover of the *Nashville Scene* for its drinks issue. The drink? You guessed it—the Reveal, renamed as the "Robo Zombie," served in a large, orange robot tiki mug designed by artist Bryce McLeod of Isle of Printing, and packing a punch with a potent blend of rums, lit on fire, and dusted with cinnamon sparks for a true taste of tableside entertainment. I'd had no idea of the amount of joy that fire, rum, and tropical concoctions would bring people. Here are some recipes to Zombify your next Halloween party, including a much lighter "punch version" that will give you all the flavors of the traditional Zombie without the feeling that you've suddenly become undead.

Zombie Punch

4 oz. lime juice

4 oz. grapefruit Juice

4 oz. cinnamon cordial (recipe on page 131)

4 oz. Falernum no. 2 (see recipe page 127)

8 oz. Puerto Rican rum, like Ron Barrelito

8 oz. El Dorado 5 year, or other aged rum

8 dashes aromatic bitters

2 oz. pomegranate juice

8 oz. water

Combine ingredients in a non-reactive bowl (due to the acid in the citrus juices), and whisk or stick-blend with an immersion blender to incorporate ingredients without ice.

TO SERVE:

2 limes, sliced into wheels and studded with cloves

2 lemons, sliced into wheels and studded with mint

1 large block of ice: Fill a large Tupperware bowl with water and a few hard spices (cinnamon, star anise) and place in the freezer. Before your party, set the Tupperware out on the counter for 15 to 20 minutes to temper, then slide the ice into your punch before serving.

In the punchbowl you'll be serving from, combine punch with the studded sliced lemons, limes, and ice block. Add more ice as needed. If anyone complains about it not being as strong as a real Zombie, stab them in the ey—wait, I mean: let them add a floater of high-proof rum (Plantations OFTD is the ideal choice), take their car keys, and say "you're welcome."

Falernum no. 2

1 bottle (750 ml) Taylor's Velvet Falernum

Zest of 2 limes

2 tablespoons ginger, peeled and chopped to small dice

10 cloves

2 allspice berries, crushed

2 oz. Wray and Nephew Overproof Rum

Pour the falernum into a Mason jar or quart deli container and add the rest of the ingredients. Shake to incorporate and set in the refrigerator to infuse for 4 days, shaking every day or so to agitate the ingredients together. Strain when finished; bottle, and keep in the refrigerator. It will stay fresh and vibrant for 2 months, and will keep for 6 months.

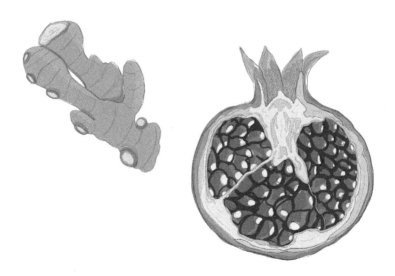

Robo Zombie AKA The Reveal

1 oz. El Dorado 5 year rum

1 oz. Jamaican rum (Hamilton, Appleton Estate, or anything funky)

1 oz. Plantation OFTD

½ oz. lime juice

½ oz. lemon juice

½ oz. Guava Falernum (see page 129)

½ oz. Fassionola (see page 129)

1 teaspoon absinthe

2 dashes exotic bitters (see page 143)

1 cup crushed ice

Flaming lime bowl, lemon oil-soaked crouton, dusted with cinnamon

Garnish: 1 sprig mint

Add all ingredients (save for garnish) to a blender and blend on high speed for 6 seconds. Pour into a long, tall glass or vessel and add ice to fill. Garnish with the mint and—should you dare—a flaming lime bowl.

Guava Falernum

2 guavas, fully ripened (available at Latin grocery stores)

1 oz. water

1 cup Falernum no. 2

1 teaspoon grated nutmeg

In a saucepan, add the water and the guavas and bring up to medium heat. Turn down to low after 5 minutes as the water evaporates, and add the Falernum no. 2. Let the falernum and guavas cook on low for 10 minutes, then remove from heat. Grate the nutmeg over the top of the mixture. Let the stewed guavas infuse in the falernum with the nutmeg in the refrigerator overnight, or longer for a more intense flavor. Strain and bottle. Kept in the refrigerator, it will keep for 1 month.

Fassionola

1 cup strawberries, washed and halved, tops left on

2 kiwis, diced

Zest and juice of 2 limes

2 cups sugar

1 cup water

8 oz. passion-fruit cordial, (recipe on page 132) for later

Combine strawberries, kiwi, lime zest and juice, sugar, and water in a saucepan and bring to a simmer, stirring to dissolve the sugar. Press on the fruit with a wooden spoon to extract as much flavor as possible. Simmer for 20 minutes on medium-low and promptly remove from heat. Transfer to the refrigerator, add the passion-fruit cordial, and allow the ingredients to infuse in the syrup overnight. Strain the next day, and bottle. Kept in the refrigerator, the cordial will keep for one month. Add an ounce of vodka or white rum to extend shelf life by 2 months.

Classic/
Beachcomber
Zombie

1½ oz. Puerto Rican rum (Ron Barrelito is a great choice for this one)

1½ oz. Jamaican rum (Hamilton or Appleton Estate)

1 oz. Plantation OFTD rum (140 proof)

½ oz. Falernum no. 2

¼ oz. cinnamon cordial (page 131)

¼ oz. fresh white grapefruit juice (sub any fresh grapefruit juice if white isn't available)

¾ oz. lime juice

1 teaspoon absinthe

1 teaspoon grenadine (page 131)

1 dash exotic bitters

1 cup crushed ice

Garnish: 1 sprig mint

Add all ingredients (except mint) to a blender, and blend on high speed for 6 to 8 seconds. Pour into a long, tall glass or vessel, and garnish with the mint sprig. Add ice cubes to fill the glass. Notice how the drink changes as it dilutes. It may taste quite strong at first (because it is!) but will have you under its spell in no time. As the legend goes, you only need one of these.

Cinnamon Cordial

1 cup crushed cinnamon

2 cups sugar

2 cups water

1 star anise pod

2 dashes aromatic bitters

In a mortar and pestle, crush enough cinnamon for 1 cup. In a saucepan, combine all ingredients and bring to a boil. Once boiling, turn down the heat to a hard simmer for 15 minutes. After 15 minutes, turn down to a low simmer, cover, and let cook for 20 minutes. This will cook off the alcohol in the bitters and thicken the syrup nicely. Let the cinnamon infuse in the syrup for 2 days in the refrigerator, then strain and bottle. It will keep for a month in the refrigerator. Add an ounce of vodka, whiskey, or rum (whichever spirit you're most likely to use with it) to extend the shelf life by 2 months.

Floral Grenadine

1 cup pomegranate juice

1 cup sugar

2 tablespoons pomegranate molasses (available at many Asian grocery stores)

Zest of 1 orange

4 drops orange flower water

4 drops rosewater

In a saucepan, combine the pomegranate juice, sugar, and molasses, and bring to a simmer, stirring to dissolve the sugar. Once dissolved, promptly remove from heat and allow to cool. Add the orange zest. Once completely cool, add the flower waters. Bottled and kept in the refrigerator, the grenadine will keep for a month. Add 1 ounce of vodka to extend shelf life by 2 months.

Pineapple Zombie

1 oz. Plantation Pineapple rum

1 oz. Jamaican rum (Hamilton or Apple Estate)

½ oz. Plantation OFTD

½ oz. Falernum no. 2

½ oz. passion-fruit cordial (see below)

1½ oz. pineapple juice

¾ oz. lime juice

1 teaspoon absinthe

1 dash exotic bitters

1 cup crushed ice

Garnish: sprig of mint; slice of pineapple

Add all ingredients (save for the garnish) to a blender and blend on high speed for 6 seconds. Pour into a long, tall glass, and add ice to fill. Garnish with a sprig of mint and a slice of pineapple. Umbrella optional.

Passion-fruit Cordial

1 cup passion-fruit puree (try the brand Perfect Puree)

2 cups sugar

2 cups water

Juice of one lemon

1 teabag Republic of Tea Passionfruit-Papaya black tea

In a saucepan combine the puree, sugar, water, and lemon juice and bring to a simmer, stirring to dissolve the sugar. Once dissolved, remove from heat and add the tea bag. Leave the tea bag in the cordial and place in the refrigerator for 8 hours, or overnight. The next day, remove the tea bag, and bottle the cordial. Kept in the refrigerator, the cordial will keep for a month. Add an ounce of vodka or white rum to extend shelf life by 2 months.

Pumpkin Zombie

1 oz. Jamaican rum

1 oz. Puerto Rican rum

½ oz. Plantation OFTD

½ oz. orange juice

1 oz. pineapple juice

½ oz. lime juice

¾ oz. pumpkin-infused vermouth (see page 102)

1 barspoon pumpkin cordial (see page 100)

¼ oz. Creole Shrubb (orange liqueur—sub Cointreau or other orange liqueur if you can't find it)

¼ oz. persimmon demerara (see page 85)

1 dash exotic bitters (see page 143)

Garnish: sprig of mint; slice of pineapple or pumpkin

Add all ingredients (save for the garnish) to a blender, and blend on high speed for 6 seconds. Pour into a long, tall glass and add ice to fill. Garnish with the mint and the pineapple or pumpkin. Umbrella optional.

Booze News ZOMBIES, FLORIDA FILES

ZOMBIES IN FLORIDA

In May of 2018, residents of Palm Beach, Florida, received an alarming text message just before 2:00 a.m. that read, "power outage and zombie alert for residents of Lake Worth and Terminus." I don't know about you, but I think Terminus sounds like a terrifying name for a town even without Zombies. The alert continued in all capital letters, which we don't do so as not to trigger you, dear reader: "There are now less than seven thousand three hundred and eighty customers involved due to extreme zombie activity. Restoration time uncertain." Later that morning, a community Facebook corrected the error, saying the message was unintended. Ben Kerr, the city's public information officer, said, "I want to reiterate that Lake Worth does not have any zombie activity currently and apologize for the system message." Palm Beach does, however, have at least three tiki bars and reviews of the local Zombie cocktails can be summed up as "terrifyingly strong."

CDC PREPARES CITIZENS FOR ZOMBIE APOCALYPSE

The Centers for Disease Control and Prevention (CDC) have had a busy few years. So I guess we have to forgive them for trying some humor on the American people, who seem to be losing their sense of humor with each passing election. While updating the public on ever-changing guidelines regarding the COVID-19 pandemic, the CDC took things a step further by offering tips for surviving a zombie apocalypse. "You may laugh now, but when it happens you'll be happy you read this," the actual CDC wrote on its website. "And hey," they continued nonchalantly, "maybe you'll even learn a thing or two about how to prepare for a real emergency." They recommend that people should prepare a kit in order to assist in case of an emergency. The kit should have a gallon of water per day for each person in your household, nonperishable food items; medications, tools and supplies; sanitation and hygiene products; clothing and bedding; important documents; and first aid supplies. At Liquid Gold, we can understand how they left rum and falernum off the list, but if you don't have a hip flask of tequila in case of emergency, god help you.

SOME OTHER TIKI TIME RECIPES FOR YOUR ZOMBIE HALLOWEEN BASH

TOASTED SPICE TEPACHE

If you're going to be working with pineapples, don't worry about "sustainability guilt" when you start throwing out all your spent pineapple rinds from juicing or garnishing. There's the traditional Mexican staple, tepache, a refreshing mildly fermented beverage made from pineapple rinds, cinnamon, clove, nutmeg, and demerara sugar. You can use this "pineapple champagne" in any holiday punch, or to increase yield *and flavor* on batched cocktails. In addition to pineapple, you can add the waste from other fruit, like banana peels, to complement the flavor of your tepache. I like toasting the spices before using them in the tepache for added backbone, especially around the holidays.

Toasted Spices

3 cinnamon sticks, crushed with the back of a skillet

5 star anise pods

1 teaspoon dried allspice berries

10 cloves

Toast spices in a skillet over medium-low heat for 5 to 10 minutes or until fragrant, swirling the pan so as not to over-toast the spices. Remove from heat and transfer the spices into a bowl to cool (cooling them in the pan may over-toast or burn them).

Toasted Spice Tepache

Rinds and leftover fruit from 2 pineapples

3 quarts water

Toasted spice blend

1½ cups demerara (turbinado) sugar

Garnish: lime wedges

Rinse the pineapple rinds and lightly pat dry with a paper towel. Combine all ingredients in a large container or pitcher, cover with cheesecloth or loosely with plastic wrap to allow fermentation, and let sit on your countertop overnight. Skim the scum (white foamy stuff) off the top of it the next day. Continue to let sit for another 2 to 3 days. Strain and filter through a fresh piece of cheesecloth. To serve, pour over ice and garnish with lime wedges. If bottling, leave in the refrigerator and use within 5 days.

Pineapple Negroni Punch

Serves 6

6 oz. Campari or other bitter orange liqueur

4½ oz. Cocchi Torino vermouth

6 oz. Plantation Pineapple rum

3 oz. pineapple juice

1½ oz. Anise Demerara Syrup (see recipe below)

1 teaspoon or 12 drops saline

Garnish: slice of fresh pineapple; star anise pod

Combine ingredients in a large pitcher or punch bowl and stir or whisk to incorporate. To serve, fill glasses with crushed or cracked ice, and garnish with a slice of fresh pineapple and a star anise pod.

Anise Demerara Syrup

2 cups turbinado "Sugar in the Raw" sugar

1 cup water

2 tablespoons crushed star anise pods (wrap in a towel and crush with the bottom of a skillet)

Combine ingredients in a saucepan and bring to a boil. Immediately turn the heat down to a low simmer and gently cook for 20 minutes. Remove from heat and allow to cool while the star anise infuses into the syrup. Once completely cooled, strain out the star anise and store the syrup in a container with a tight-fitting lid. Kept in the refrigerator, the syrup will last for about a month.

Always Summer Pineapple Negroni

1 oz. Campari or other bitter orange liqueur

¾ oz. Cocchi Torino vermouth

1 oz. Plantation Pineapple rum

½ oz. pineapple juice

1 teaspoon Anise Demerara Syrup (see recipe page 138)

1 tiny pinch salt, or 2 drops saline

Garnish: slice of fresh pineapple; star anise pod

Build in a glass full of crushed ice and gently jostle as you add the ingredients. Garnish with a slice of fresh pineapple and a star anise pod.

Homemade Allspice Liqueur

1 32-oz Mason jar

1 cup allspice berries

2 cinnamon sticks

1 (750 ml) bottle Hamilton Jamaican Gold Rum (or other Jamaican rum, for the funky banana aroma)

1 cup demerara sugar

1 cup water

Crush the cinnamon sticks and allspice berries in a mortar and pestle until broken up. Combine the rum and the broken-up cinnamon and allspice into the quart Mason jar and seal. Shake briskly and store in a cool place away from sunlight. Shake daily for a week. After a week, taste the mixture and see how your flavors are melding. You only want the cinnamon to embolden and diversify the allspice flavor, which you want to be pronounced since you won't be using much of it per drink. Add more crushed allspice if needed. Let the mixture sit for another week, shaking it whenever you can. After a few weeks (or less, if you're happy with the flavor), it'll be time to sweeten the liqueur. Strain out the allspice and cinnamon from the jar with cheesecloth or a tea strainer, and set aside to use in the syrup you're about to make. In a saucepan, combine the demerara sugar, water, and spices, and bring to a boil. Once boiling, turn down to a simmer for 15 minutes, then remove from heat and allow to cool. Once cooled, strain out the spices and add the syrup to the jar and shake to incorporate. Allow the liqueur to rest for a few days. Bottle (or store in the Mason jar) and keep in the refrigerator. The liqueur will keep for 3 months.

Exotic Bitters

1 pint Mason jar

2 cinnamon sticks

2 tablespoons allspice berries

2 whole nutmegs

3 star anise pods

20 cloves

1 teaspoon gentian root

1 tablespoon cassia buds

1 bourbon vanilla pod

16 oz. Wray and Nephew Overproof Rum

½ cup demerara sugar

½ cup water

Crush the cinnamon, allspice, nutmeg, and star anise together in a mortar and pestle until broken up. Add them—along with the cloves, gentian, cassia buds, and vanilla—to a pint Mason jar and top with the rum. Store in a cool place away from sunlight, and shake daily (or as much as you can) for 2 weeks. Taste after a few weeks and see how the flavors are melding. For a stronger flavor, keep the infusion going for another 2 weeks. Once the infusion is to your liking, strain out the solids from the pint Mason jar and set them aside to use in the syrup. In a saucepan combine the sugar, water, and strained spices, and bring to a boil. Once boiling, lower heat immediately to a simmer for 20 minutes. Strain out the spices and let the syrup cool completely. Once cooled, add to the bitters mixture a tablespoon at a time until you're happy with the taste. You want heavy spice character, mild bitterness, and a little sweetness to make your bitters delicious and easy to work with. Bottled in a dark dropper bottle, these bitters will keep for a year.

Fall Mai Tai

2 oz. Jamaican rum

½ oz. Rhum Martinique (Neisson or Clement would be a great choice)

¾ oz. lime juice

½ oz. chai tea (see page 118)

½ oz. Falernum no. 2 (see page 127)

Scant ¼ oz. Creole Shrub (orange liqueur)

1 barspoon orange juice

1 barspoon persimmon demerara (see page 85)

1 dash exotic bitters

Garnish: 1 lime hull; 1 sprig mint

Shake all ingredients with equal amounts crushed and cubed ice and open-pour into a double old-fashioned glass and garnish with the lime hull and mint.

Blood orange Mai Tai

2 slices blood orange

1½ oz. El Dorado 5 year rum

½ oz. Rhum Martinique

¾ oz. lime juice

½ oz. chai tea (see page 118)

½ oz. Falernum no. 2 (see page 127)

1 barspoon sweet vermouth (Corsican or Dolin would be great)

1 dash exotic bitters

Garnish: 1 slice blood orange, halved; 1 sprig mint

Muddle 1 orange slice at the bottom of your shaker tin. Then add a cup of crushed or cubed ice along with the rest of the ingredients, and shake vigorously. Double strain into an old-fashioned or mai tai glass and garnish with a slice of blood orange and a sprig of mint.

Dr. Funkenstein

1 oz. Jamaican rum

1 oz. gin

1 barspoon Green Chartreuse

¾ oz. lime juice

½ oz. allspice liqueur (see page 141)

1 barspoon persimmon demerara (see page 85)

1 teaspoon absinthe

1 cup crushed ice

Topping: Peychaud's bitters

Garnish: 1 sprig mint

Add rum, gin, chartreuse, lime juice, allspice liqueur, demerara, absinthe, and ice to a blender and blend for 6 seconds. Serve in a tall glass or vessel and garnish with a sprig of mint, dashing Peychaud's bitters on top for a "blood effect."

THE CARIBBEAN OLD-FASHIONED VARIATION THAT IS THE PERFECT ANTI-TIKI DRINK

One of our favorite guests we've ever had on the show—rum blender and trailblazer Ed Hamilton—knows a thing or two about the rhum agricoles of Martinique, *the* rhum responsible for the Tí Punch. These younger, perfumely pungent, lemongrassy spirits are a gorgeous counterpart to the rich, robust aged rums of Jamaica, Guyana, and throughout the Caribbean. Delicious and strong on their own, they become open and alive when mixed into a Tí Punch, the lime acting like a ray of sunshine cutting across the glass and mingling with a little ice. "It allows the rhum to blossom," said Ed one afternoon as we sipped a few Tí punches in the studio.

Tí Punch

This is more a method than a recipe, more of a lifestyle choice than any kind of kitschy tropical beverage. This is for all your friends who just don't like fun—er, I mean tiki drinks. If we're being real, though, isn't a simple old-fashioned what everyone wants now and then? This drink is three ingredients and the truth.

IN AN OLD-FASHIONED GLASS, COMBINE:

2 peels of lime that have fruit the diameter of a nickel with the depth of a poker chip.

Add a dash of angostura bitters and ¼ oz. of rich demerara syrup, or other rich syrup of your choice. Muddle ingredients with ease. Add 2 oz. of Rhum Clement Blanc or other Rhum Agricole, add ice, and stir briskly until the drink is nice and cold, garnishing with lime peel.

Booze News TIKI, FLORIDA FILES

TIKI BAR LITERALLY LOST OUT TO SEA

NBC news in Key West recounted that a floating tiki bar, reported stolen earlier in the week, was found by the Coast Guard, complete with an intoxicated passenger onboard, the likely culprit. "We'd like to remind mariners not to drink and boat," commented the Coast Guard. A local Fox News affiliate added: "It remains unclear whether the suspect had been drinking Mai Tais, Hurricanes, or something else." However, if we're taking into account the setting of Key West, we're guessing it was one too many Mojitos. Which, come to think of it, would make a good Jimmy Buffet song.

STRANDED MAN PRAYS FOR HELP, SAVED BY TIKI BAR PRIESTS

Fox News in Albany reported that a man named Jimmy MacDonald, stranded and lost in thirty-foot-deep water in upstate New York as wind ravaged his kayak, was saved by the Paulist Fathers, a Catholic religious group from St. Joseph's Seminary in Washington, DC. The group of Seminarians were on a "Tiki Tours" boat when they spotted the man in need. "I just take that as a sign from God that he's got me here for a real reason," said MacDonald. Commenters on the article online bemoaned the lack of any photographic evidence of the floating tiki bar. User "JIMMYBEAMER" commented, "I ONLY scrolled to see the tiki bar. Disappointed." Another added, "Why didn't he take a photo of the tiki bar?" We're just wondering what on earth you serve to priests who are taking in the sights on a floating tiki bar. Non-alcoholic piña coladas is our best guess.

FIVE

A Spooky Season Short Story— "Who Cooks for You?"

We backed out of the driveway slowly, in the old auburn Ford Taurus station wagon my parents had been driving me to camp in every summer for the last four years.

They were bickering over how much gas was in the tank and who had driven it last, when my dad turned over his right shoulder, bringing his hairy arm over the passenger seat, his left hand slowly winding the wheel as he suddenly hit the brakes—

"Shitsticks!" he gasped as my mom white-knuckled the dashboard in front of her and a familiar black Trans Am went speeding down our street.

"Jesus, not again," said my mom as her breath returned.

"That kid drives like a bat outta hell! I couldn't even hear his engine with you screaming in my ear about the goddamn gas gauge," said Dad, still not even out of the driveway.

"I'll talk to his mom. You know we haven't been over there since Memorial Day when all those brats on the grill flamed up and nearly singed off your beard," said Mom, her innate ability to conjure up an embarrassing moment to suit any situation for Dad still intact.

The three-and-a-half-hour drive to Camp Kokomo, deep in the wild, southwestern corner of the Smoky Mountains, always seemed to take twice as long. I leafed through my new used copy of "Native Plants of the Smoky Mountains" until my stomach turned sour and every slight change in the road made me feel more carsick. I gently cracked the window to let some air through my hair and allowed my eyes to wander through the verdant hills surrounding both sides of the road, as we barreled our way through the outskirts of Knoxville.

"You okay back there, sweetie?" said Mom, who, when I was much younger, used to have to bend her way to the back seat to hand me the extra Big Gulp cup every time I thought I was about to lose my lunch on a long car ride.

"Yeah, I think so," I said, unsure if I was getting too old to play up a sickness or not.

It's not like I'd get to miss any school or anything. I was headed to camp, where, if you weren't feeling well, you either had to stay away from the other kids or stay the night in the medical tent, where the cots seemed to have missing joints, like sleeping on a clothesline.

I pondered my parents from the back seat, Dad's hair in full October, colors changing and blending, slowly falling out with a bright harvest-moon bald spot in the middle of his head, thankfully unnoticed by many a camera. My mom's tan, sandy blond locks, like the beaches of the Gulf after it rains, carefully calibrated by her hairstylist Amanda, who came to the house to play bridge, drink wine spritzers, and smoke 100's on the back deck. I looked at Dad's leather watch and his hands on the wheel and thought about how I couldn't wait to start driving. I was quite certain I'd be going fifteen over what my dad was doing, who felt the need to opine, on every road trip, "If we go any faster, we're killing our gas mileage."

I glanced back down at my book at both the picture and the illustration of *daucus carota*—wild carrot—and felt a twinge of both excitement and dread, as my "season of study" was to focus on the identification of native flora—which I had been fascinated with since the day I kissed Katy, literally the girl next door, in the back yard after sucking on the honeysuckle nectar from the overflowing vines billowing over the fence behind my neighbor's carport. "The Great Smoky Mountains," as the book denoted had always been an education in terms of wildlife, and I was looking forward to not being on the constant lookout for bears, who had become boring to me at thirteen years old. I was entranced not by the sudden force of wild animals who lurked in silences across the great foggy ridges, but by the magic held within the cell walls of the exotic and unknown plants of these majestic mountains.

I also loved to cook, mostly garlic mac 'n' cheese—"have one dish," Mom always told me—and the head counselor had promised me I could assist in the canteen that year, probably my last, as an assistant to the cooks who labored over green beans, squash casserole, lima beans with bacon, and, when we were lucky, fried chicken. This meant I needed to cozy up to the one person I was terrified of every summer at camp: Suzy Salinger, or, as we called her, Suzy the Slayer. Suzy was the head cook at camp. She had become so tired of kids making fun of her lazy eye over the years that it was rumored she had poisoned a few children by adding cyanide to their sweet tea. I was never able to confirm this with anyone, though some of the older custodians at camp would just shake their heads and mutter "Suzy crazy, boy, don't you go messin' with that woman."

Suzy had grown up with four brothers in the shadow of Black Mountain in the southwest corner of Kentucky coal-mine country, the only daughter to her mom—a descendant of the Cherokee who had been in the area for centuries—and her dad who worked the coal mines and taught her how to play fiddle by a campfire. She had long black hair with a few white streaks, like lightning hung on a dark sky or the veins of white running across a skunk's back. Her tall, slender frame slid across the kitchen without a sound, before traipsing down the mess hall line to see what was getting low, then through the dining area to glare at the campers who either complained about the food or—as they often did but almost never followed through on—quietly threatened a food fight by shooting mischievous glares around the room and faking sudden, ill-conceived throwing motions.

"Are these the beans from last week?" someone would call out anonymously while Suzy's back was turned. She seemed to have eyes in those white streaks in the back of her hair.

"Last year, maybe!" yelled another kid from the next table over.

"Who cooks for you?" she'd whip around and say, like a serpent looking for her prey. "Who cooks for all of you?" she'd say, motioning around the room. That was her trademark, the soliloquy that became her rallying cry. Word was, she used to say it all the time under her breath before she just couldn't keep it in any longer and started hissing the words to any camper who dared to criticize her food or complain about the lack of variation in the menu.

Since I was one of the older kids that year, my room was a double, and I shared it with none other than TG, Tommy George Swanson, a troublemaker I'd known since we were six, who loved to play with fire, could outrun the kids in high school when he shot fireworks at their cars, and almost broke his neck trying to flip off a dirt hill on his bike when we were ten years old. To say he had a propensity for danger and risk would be putting it mildly.

"Do you realize how many black cat fireworks fit into one of those huge orange pylons behind the dumpster?" he once said to me at the foot of a large elm tree. "It's basically a small bomb. It's like baseball game fireworks."

TG got the bright idea one night, after everyone else had gone to bed and the only sound coming through the screen in our window was a coyote about a mile away near Blackstone Lake, that we needed to sneak into the cafeteria kitchen and steal some ice cream. To escape possible detection, we followed a group of shadows from our bunkhouse to the mess hall, avoiding the slanted pockets of light that angled across the camp courtyard like a picture frame hanging askew. I used my key to get us through the side entrance, up the ramp and down the hallway to the cafeteria. Out the wide but rectangularly narrow windows by the exit doors I saw a flash of light, then seconds later I heard the first metallic drops of rain begin to fall on a tin roof across the courtyard. Then I felt a sudden rush of cold run from the tips of the hair on my arm shooting straight through to my bones, like the time I died in a dream. Then the touch of long, slender fingers with sharp nails was grasping my neck—not choking, more handling it like a Styrofoam cup of coffee—and I immediately froze and slowly turned my head. TG was walking ahead of me softly and didn't hear a thing, so he kept on.

"Wha' the—?" I murmured, surprised to have a breath. The hand around my neck fell and grazed my shoulder.

"Give me that key, you little mouse!" said Suzy, towering over me, her black hair shading her face. "Scurrying around in here in the dark, looking for . . . What are y'all lookin for, anyway?"

TG froze like a turkey in the rain. "Iiiii . . . ice cream," he blurted out with a quiver in his voice.

"Ice cream, huh? You don't sneak into my kitchen late at night . . . or ever, come to think of it!" She walked slowly over to TG and extended her index finger. Her nails were freshly painted black, shining like the hood of a hearse that had just been washed. She pointed at him for what seemed like days, as time hung on the wall and TG's eyes widened. Then she put her finger under his chin and tilted his head up to look her square in the eyes.

"I'm sorry, Suzy, we'll go ahead and get outta yer hair," was the only thing TG could think to say. He jerked his neck a little as if to move.

"Youuuuu! Don't move," she called out in the empty cafeteria. "You're going to help me cook tonight. I'm starting a stew and it needs to cook for fourteen hours. It'll be ready by lunch tomorrow if we get to it. Now come on."

She looked at me with mild disgust and motioned for us to follow her into the kitchen. Her movements immediately became quick and decisive as she flipped on the lights and tossed an apron over her neck, tying it as she glanced around the room. I knew to immediately fetch the big stockpot sitting upside down on the shelf next to the dishwasher.

"You get the carrots washed and peeled," she said to me. "Tommy, put some latex gloves on, you're going to help me chop the meat." Tommy barely knew how to make a sandwich, but he loved knives, and I wondered if the first-aid kit was still in the same place in the kitchen. Suzy walked over to the radio resting on the windowsill and switched it on, soft and low. Her long black fingernail scraped the radio slightly as she dialed in a country station, playing Hank Williams's "Kaw-Liga." Rain continued to fall outside the window, and I thought about my dad as I turned the cold steel knob on the sink.

It was the kind of mindless work that set a mind to wander. If it had been any other night, we'd be eating ice cream right now. As Suzy plopped a cutting board down and began peeling onions, TG, as instructed, filled up a pitcher with Coca-Cola from a few 2-liter bottles. Suzy sliced through the onions like a samurai, moving on to the celery as she drilled TG around the room to do only the simplest tasks.

"Go turn that middle knob on the stove on and ignite the gas with the lighter in your side pocket," Suzy said. How she knew he had a lighter remains a mystery to me. TG cranked the knob to let out the gas and reached for his lighter. As he drew it from the cargo pocket on his right leg, he fumbled, and the lighter tumbled to the clean, hard linoleum floor with a plastic clatter. He dropped to the floor quickly and retrieved it from just under the stove and popped back up to light the burner. There must have been firework residue on his right arm from the black cats we'd shot off a few hours earlier, as a huge burst of flame roared out from the stovetop and set most of Tommy's arm on fire. It brought upon the sterile, fluorescent lighting of the room a bold burst of color, and I admit to being transfixed by the sight for a second before the shriek of his screams sent me into action.

"Aggghhhhh!!!" yelled Tommy.

"Shit! Grab the baking soda and throw some on his arm," said Suzy as she darted over to Tommy.

We had a few clear plastic containers—the tall thin ones that I'd seen hippy parents keep their cereal in—that were labeled BAKING SODA, FLOUR, SUGAR, and so on. Now, I knew the baking soda container was the small one with the tight-fitting lid, but in my panic I somehow managed to grab the container of flour and popped the top as I ran over to Tommy. I threw a handful of flour toward his blazing arm, fearing I had made a mistake as the white dust flew through the air, while I noticed Suzy's eyes bulge and her nostrils flare in terror. With the fire-igniting dusting of flour, the flames on Tommy's arm suddenly became a fireball that reached to the ceiling, as Suzy flung off her apron and quickly outstretched it as if hanging a sheet on a clothesline. She dove toward Tommy and wrapped the apron around his right side, tackling him to the floor. She began tamping out the fire while I removed my flannel shirt and attempted to do the same. Tommy—in shock—though I imagined deep down he had to be impressed by the pyrotechnics of the event— moaned a terrifyingly raspy drone that oscillated as he rocked sideways on the floor. The fire was out, and, oddly, the room smelled very similar to the last time Suzy had made beef stew. I looked at her with eyes that said "I'm sorry," and my cheek began to twitch.

"Tommy, uhhh . . . you okay, man?"

Suzy peeled away the apron and coat to reveal Tommy's charred, discolored right arm. It looked like the painting of a mental patient, yellow and black spots with blue and red blotches. Smoke lifted like fog coming off the lake in the early morning.

"Burning flesh really smells like beef fat," she said, shooting me a look of exasperation and, for the first time in the three years I'd known her, uncertainty. "Go get the ice cream." She motioned me away. Lights flickered on in the courtyard as Camp Kokomo stirred in the night.

* * * * * * * * *

Weeks later, as I walked with Suzy through the tangled woods beyond camp searching for mushrooms to be used in a soup, I thought of Tommy and wondered if his arm was healing back home. He had been sent home the day after cooking his arm in the kitchen, diagnosed with second-degree burns, while Suzy took most of the heat for having a thirteen-year-old with a pyro problem light a gas stove at what was supposed to be lights-out time. The kids at camp had built the story up and bent the facts to fit their imaginations, speculating that Suzy had orchestrated the whole thing on purpose. Instead of my own ineptitude being the reason for escalating the fire, many suspicions that Suzy was in fact a witch with magical powers began to infiltrate the nighttime stories and flashlight follies around the campfires and bed bunks. As I watched her gracefully swoop down to snip mushrooms from their earthbound cots, her hair swaying back and forth like the lazy branches of a weeping willow, I began to see her as a genuine fairy in the forest. She had a graceful way of doing the simplest of things and made the most mundane activities seem so interesting.

Back at camp that night, the cafeteria was typically chaotic before dinner, with spitballs flying and inexplicable screams of laughter. I began passing out baskets of bread as Suzy put the final touches on the cream-of-mushroom soup in the kitchen. As she emerged from the kitchen, an unwise camper sent a spitball straight at Suzy's lazy eye with such force that it ricocheted off her eyeball and into one of the bowls of soup on her tray. Suzy froze as her dark, tanned complexion turned blood-red. She glanced down at the soup bowl with the spitball in it and watched as the wet ball of paper descended into the soup. She flung around without spilling a drop and turned back into the kitchen, as I searched the room for the culprit. The cafeteria began to fall silent as Melissa, a counselor in her first year at camp, walked around the tables with her arms folded and eyes piercing. Suzy emerged from the kitchen and began dispersing the soup as though nothing had happened, while I sulked back to the kitchen to heat up more bread. When I peeked out into the cafeteria from the circular glass window on the swinging kitchen door, I saw an otherworldly sight: Suzy's long wooden spoon had caught fire, and she was wielding it like a weapon as she leapt onto one of the tables and motioned around the room like a conductor at the symphony.

"Who cooks for you?" she screamed at one table. "Who cooks for you all?"

All the kids began to double over in pain and fall to the floor, shrinking in size before my eyes and suddenly turning into mice! Other counselors began to pass out from the shock as Suzy jumped down from the table and stormed toward Melissa, who sat in a chair shaking, her red, curly hair turning white and gray as she morphed into a cat and immediately ran off. Terrified, I ran across to the other door and attempted an escape out the back. I heard an ungodly shriek; and as I turned back, I noticed a plume of smoke lifting toward the high ceiling of the cafeteria. An owl with a white streak down its side emerged from the smoke, as I turned to run out the back door. Mice began to scurry everywhere, following me out the back. I heard a window break with a thundering shatter, as a stockpot clanged on the ground and the owl came flying out the window with great force, finally resting its talons on one of the power lines adjacent to the courtyard. As I hid behind a sturdy, bear-proof trash can, I glanced around its corner and saw the owl descending down into the courtyard, plucking the mice off the ground with its large talons and flinging them across the yard. A voice back in the cafeteria let out a terrifying scream. I slowly backed away, careful not to fall, keeping a close eye on the owl who let out its blood-curdling call:

"Who cooks for you, who cooks for you all!"

SIX

Agavember— The Wide World of Agave Drinks

Let's face it: tequila is unfair. Maybe you've heard us labor over the point before.

No other spirit—unless you want to argue about another agave spirit like Mezcal or Raicilla—gives you the same feeling of life coursing through your veins the way tequila does. No other spirit can claim to be a stimulant *and the reason why Sammy Haggar still matters.* But before I start writing another country song about the pleasures and pain of tequila, let's look at the components and break down why these agave spirits are so well-suited to drinks.

+ Salt makes everything taste better and is a key ingredient in everyday sweets like ice cream. It's also incredible with tequila and an essential component to almost *any tequila drink.* Salt and tequila belong together. Completely unfair to other spirits around the world.

+ Tequila has three basic categories or aging systems: blanco (unaged or "rested" for 1 month), reposado (aged from 2 months to 1 year), and anejo (aged 1 to 5 years), while some brands are experimenting with extra anejos that are aged as long as 9 years. What's unfair is how all are delicious in their own ways (rare in the spirit world) and all go with a wide variety of ingredients, from summer and exotic fruits to vermouths and amaros. Ever heard a spirits professional wax poetic about how the real subtleties of whiskey reside in the unaged, pure expression of moonshine? Yeah, me neither. I'd say it's kind of unfair.

+ Another flavor-enhancer ingredient that makes most foods it comes in contact with decidedly more delicious: hot peppers and spice. Tequila and other agave-based spirits are like thunder to the spicy-pepper lightning, and when the two are mixed together, there are fireworks. Or maybe that's the heartburn? Still unfair.

+ It's actually better than vodka in a bloody mary, for many of the reasons listed above. If we're to square up to any debate involving heavy hitters such as vodka and tequila, we must admit that vodka, without the heft of deft marketing thrown behind it, is supposed to taste as neutral as possible. Not delicious, but neutral. Doesn't seem like a fair fight to us.

+ You can crisscross seasons with tequila. Barrel-aged and warming, even a hot tequila toddy, to a cucumber margarita with the first pick of the spring strawberries. Later in the summer: watermelon and basil with mint. Fall spices with reposado? Sign me up, though it all seems unfair.

+ Tequila brings out the truth in people and has been used in interrogation (by ex-husbands and -wives). Truth serum, tequila . . . both have three syllables, one can only guess why.

+ The most ubiquitous cordial in the world of mixed drinks, other than simple syrup, is grenadine. Though nearly destroyed during the darkest days of the cocktail in the late '70s and '80s, when it became an imitation of itself as it languished on grocery store shelves, real-pomegranate grenadine is back to being the bar staple it always was. While the artificial versions were made with ingredients like corn syrup and red food coloring—whose only real purpose in life was to make Shirley Temples—bartenders are creative with grenadine now, combining pomegranate molasses with pomegranate juice and flower waters (page 56) to create exotic, aromatic cocktails. The spirit most suited to grenadine, from a pomegranate flavor-affinity standpoint? That's right, tequila by a mile. Hardly fair.

+ I mentioned hot peppers and their relation to tequila but what about other vegetables like celery, cucumber, squash, and corn? Can you think of any spirit that even remotely works with these oft-forgotten ingredients of the beverage lexicon? I'll wait . . . Tequila, in fact, is ideal with all these fresh, singular flavors. Fucking unfair.

Through all this hyperbole, tequila actually has something quite unfair to contend with in the wide world of spirits, where everything we drink

is connected to the natural world in some fashion. Just as good whiskey, made from a mash of grain from one growing season, can take anywhere from four to fifteen years to reach optimum flavor, the agave plant from which tequila is made takes anywhere from seven to ten years to reach the level of maturity needed for proper tequila distillation. In late 2014, there was even talk of a coming "tequila shortage" due to the constraints on blue agave production and harvesting. With demand increasing by 40 to 50 percent a year over the last few years, further strains on the blue agave plant are almost certain in the years to come. Just when tequila begins to scale the mountain of dominating the spirits world, there isn't enough of the raw materials to push it over the top? Sometimes it's life that isn't fair.

In the meantime, savor the many different ways to enjoy tequila in this chapter. While typically a spring and summer phenomenon, the celebration of "Dia de Los Muertos" in the United States during the first days of November usually brings a plethora of tequila and mezcal drink specials at bars everywhere. However, I think it's time to separate these two wildly different cultural cornerstones: Mexicans celebrating their loved ones who have passed on with joyful, artistic rituals; and Americans who are just excited to have another reason to crush a bunch of tequila before winter finally sets in. Dia de Los Muertos deserves its own respect and shouldn't be co-opted by liquor brands, bars, and state lottery boards, so let's just leave it at that. We can still have fun and bask in the various ways in which we enjoy the desert chameleon of spirits. Let's call it AGAVEMBER: "Tequila is the reason for the season," something like that. We can plaster it all over department stores, rural county Walmarts, even six-packs of beer. Instead of a Dia de Los Muertos sugar skull on the side of that November seasonal sixer (which serves no purpose to honor someone's *abuela* other than to shrug and say "let's party"), why not add the national AGAVEMBER logo (a stark agave plant of dubious age) and the phrase "You thought tequila drinking season was over? Think again, bitch. Don't forget to stop by the tequila aisle on your way out." Maybe we leave the "bitch" part out? What can I say, I am stimulated by all this tequila that is swirling in my glass and talking to me as if the idea of gravity itself were in question. Tequila is the truth serum that made me realize that the only truth about binging on tequila in the first two days of November is that it has very little to do with my Mexican friend's dead relatives. We can all enjoy this spirit's culture while giving proper reverence to its traditions, without stepping in to try to make them our own two-for-one special.

CITRUS BITTERS

Making your own citrus bitters can provide you with a versatile cocktail ingredient that can be used in harmony with almost any spirit or liqueur. With many classic tequila cocktails relying on the use of fresh citrus, a well-balanced citrus bitter element can provide complexity and structural backbone to the finished product. You can also experiment with tequila's long-lost pal, salt, by adding a light salinity to your bitters through the use of good sea salt. Many of the finest blanco tequilas have that aroma of ocean air, something you can lean into in your own bitters recipes.

Citrus Bitters (for Agave Drinks)

1 32-oz. Mason jar

2 star anise pods

2 cloves

15 oz. 100-proof vodka

15 oz. Blanco Tequila

1 tablespoon gentian root (available from Mountain Rose Herbs and other online retailers)

Zest of 2 oranges, dried (zest an orange and dry on a plate

on your countertop overnight)

Zest of 5 limes, dried (can use same method as orange zest)

Zest of 3 grapefruits, dried

Zest of one pomelo, dried

4 oz. agave nectar

1 tablespoon sea salt

Add the star anise and clove to a skillet over medium-low heat and toast lightly, taking care not to overcook or burn the spices. Transfer them to a plate to allow them to cool. Once cooled, add them to a 32-ounce Mason jar, along with the gentian and dried citrus zest, and let sit in a cool, dry place in your kitchen away from sunlight. As often as once a day (or a little less if the day gets away from you), shake the mixture briskly to get as much extraction from your botanicals as possible. Taste the mixture every 3 or 4 days to see how the flavor increases.

After 3 weeks, if you're happy with the extraction and intensity of the flavor, strain out the solids through cheesecloth and add the agave nectar. Then add the salt to this mixture and stir to combine. The bitters will keep for at least a year.

THE "TEQUILA IS UNFAIR" HURRICANE

As an example to lay bare the multitudinous reasons why tequila makes way more sense as the base spirit in almost *any drink with citrus in it,* we'll turn to this Hurricane riff that seeks to drag the Hurricane out of the Bourbon Street gutter in New Orleans and put it right on your back deck for a night of (safe and sensible) debauchery. If you enjoyed the previous tiki chapter but prefer tequila to rum, this drink was created just for you. When I was running a tiki bar in Nashville, I'd hear from a lot of customers: "These drinks all look great and everything, but can I have something with tequila in it?" The Tequila Hurricane was born.

Hurricane Patricia

2 oz. Exotico Blanco

¾ oz. pineapple juice

¾ oz. lime juice

½ oz. passionfruit cordial

¼ oz. grenadine

1 dash citrus bitters (page 166)

Tiny pinch salt

1 dash Angostura bitters

Garnish: pineapple frond; half orange slice

Pulse ingredients (save for the garnish) in a blender for 6 to 8 seconds, and serve in a pilsner glass, garnishing with the pineapple frond and the orange slice.

PRICKLY PEAR AND AGAVE

With Agavember set to roll out in November, there can be a limited amount of fresh produce to enjoy with your ration of tequila or other agave-based spirits. Luckily, there were a lot of hippies in the 1960s and '70s who took to the wild untamed look of the ornamental Prickly Pear cactus. What this means, whether you live in Denver, Nashville, or any of the other cities and towns where I've seen it growing, is that prickly pear is likely within reach for you. And if no one is growing it nearby, it's usually very easy to find at a good Latin grocery store. To handle and break down prickly pear, it can help to have a small torch handy to burn off the outer pricklies, which should come right off after a quick singe of heat. The fruit of prickly pear is fuschia-colored and delicious, like a cross between a fruity variety of beets, pomegranate, and unripe strawberry with bright acidity. Sounds like it's made for tequila!

Grilled Prickly Pear Cordial

1½ cups sugar

⅔ cup water

1 teaspoon distilled white vinegar

2 large, ripe prickly pears (about 10 oz.), pricklies singed with a flame and cut off and cut into quarters

1½ teaspoons grated orange zest (use a Microplane)

Combine the sugar and water in a small saucepan and bring the mixture to a simmer over medium heat, stirring to dissolve the sugar, about 5 minutes. Remove from the stove and cool to room temperature. Add the vinegar, and stir to combine. Transfer to a container or jar and set aside.

Prepare a hot grill, distributing the coals in an even layer in the bottom of the grill.

Place the prickly pear in the grill basket and place the basket directly on the coals. Grill the pears until they develop a little color, not too charred, about 3 minutes. Turn the pears over and cook on the other side until lightly charred, another 2 minutes. Transfer them to the container of syrup, add the orange zest, cover, and let the cordial cool to room temperature. Then place in the refrigerator and infuse overnight.

Strain the cordial through a fine-mesh sieve into a clean container and discard the solids. Cover and refrigerate. Tightly covered, the cordial will keep for up to 2 weeks in the refrigerator.

Prickly Pear Fermented Beverage (Colonche)

4 prickly pears, trimmed and quartered

2 cinnamon sticks

4 cloves

2 star anise pods

2 allspice berries

3 quarts water

1½ cups demerara (turbinado) sugar

Garnish: lime wedges

Prepare the prickly pears by singeing off or removing the pricklies and quartering the fruit. Toast the spices in a skillet and allow them to cool. Combine all ingredients in a large container or pitcher, cover with cheesecloth or loosely with plastic wrap to allow fermentation, and let sit on your countertop overnight. Skim the scum (white foamy stuff) off the top of it the next day. Continue to let sit for another 2 or 3 days. Strain and filter through a fresh piece of cheesecloth. To serve, pour over ice and garnish with lime wedges. If bottling, leave in the refrigerator and use within a few weeks. Fermentation will likely continue, so watch for a buildup of carbonation!

Prickly Margarita

2 oz. blanco tequila

¾ oz. lime juice

1 barspoon orange juice

¼ oz. agave nectar

½ oz. prickly pear cordial

1 dash citrus bitters

Tiny pinch of salt

Combine ingredients in a shaker with ice, and shake until well chilled. Open-pour into a rocks glass with an optional salted rim, and garnish with an orange wedge.

Prickly Paloma

2 oz. reposado tequila

½ oz. lime juice

1 oz. grapefruit juice

1 barspoon prickly pear cordial (see page 171)

1 dash citrus bitters

Tiny pinch of salt

Prickly pear "colonche", see page 172 (or pellegrino prickly pear soda)

Aleppo-salted rim

Garnish: orange wedge

Prepare the salted rim on the glass. Combine ingredients, except for colonche, in a shaker with ice. Shake until well chilled. Strain into a tall glass with ice, and top with colonche or prickly pear soda. Garnish with an orange wedge.

Sage Prickly Pear "Champagne" Cocktail

1 oz. reposado tequila

4 leaves sage

½ oz. prickly pear cordial

6 oz. prickly pear "colonche" (recipe on page 172)

Tiny pinch of salt

Garnish: fresh sage

In a mixing glass add the tequila, sage leaves, and prickly pear cordial, and muddle the sage leaves for a while. Taste to see how much you've extracted. If you're pleased with the sage flavor, add ice and salt and stir for about 15 seconds. Let the drink sit for about 4 to 5 minutes to chill and dilute, and strain into a wine glass. Top with the colonche and garnish with fresh sage.

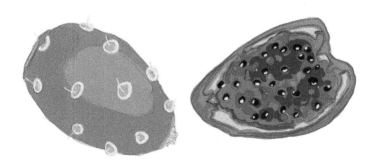

Mexico City Cocktail

2 oz. Anejo tequila

¼ oz. Prickly Pear Cordial (see page 171)

½ oz. Amaro Nonino (or other light, orange-leaning amaro)

1 dash citrus bitters

Tiny pinch salt

Garnish: star anise pod; orange peel

Stir ingredients in a mixing glass with plenty of ice until well chilled. Strain into a coupe glass and garnish with an orange peel, expressed and discarded, and a star anise pod.

Aleppo Paloma

2 oz. Blanco tequila

½ oz. lime juice

1 oz. grapefruit juice

¼ oz. agave nectar

1 dash citrus bitters

Aleppo salt rim

Mexican Squirt or Jarritos Grapefruit, to top

Garnish: half wheel lime

Prepare the salt rim on the glass. Shake ingredients, except for the Squirt or Jarritos, in a shaker with ice until chilled. Strain into a tall glass with ice, and top with Squirt or Jarritos. Garnish with a lime half wheel.

INTRODUCTION TO SOTOL

While it seems possible that we'll see tequila made in Australia some-day—due to innovations down under, turning drought-tolerant agave plants into renewable energy—it will have to be called something else, as tequila *must* be made in Mexico, specifically in Jalisco. But sotol—a spirit made in Mexico and Texas and probably elsewhere by the time this book is printed—distilled from the "Desert Spoon" cactus plant, which is actually from the asparagus family, is the new kid on the block. In fact, even though it is made in a manner similar to artisanal mezcals, and has a flavor profile akin to many agave spirits, it isn't necessarily considered an agave spirit. Lucky for us, it works with many of the same flavor profiles as agave spirits. Sotol has less smoke and intensity on the palate than many mezcals, but also has more character and complexity than most cocktail-able tequilas. On your next trip to the bottle shop, check out a bottle of sotol and see how it compares to your favorite agave spirit. For AGAVEMBER, we can make a few exceptions on which plants a spirit comes from. Enjoy these recipes featuring sotol.

Smoked Beet Sotol

3 beets, washed and peeled (be careful not to stain everything beets come in contact with)

A pinch of salt

A few turns of black pepper from a pepper grinder

1 tablespoon olive oil

1 (750 ml) bottle of sotol

Wash and peel beets, put them in tin foil with the olive oil, salt, and pepper, and place in a fire with plenty of coals on the bottom and roast in the fire for 30 minutes. Take out with tongs and place on a ceramic plate (plastic plates will get stained by the beets). Once cooled, quarter the beets and place them in a container with sotol and let infuse for a week, away from sunlight.

Sotol Beet Paloma with Nasturtium

2 oz. beet sotol (recipe page 180)

½ oz. lime juice

1 oz. grapefruit juice

¼ oz. prickly pear cordial (see page 171)

1 dash lovage bitters (see recipe below)

Celery salt rim (celery seeds, celery salt, beet powder, and sea salt)

Soda: Mexican Squirt, Jarritos Grapefruit, or colonche (to top)

Garnish: orange wedge

Prepare the salt rim on the glass and set aside. Combine all ingredients (except for the soda) in a shaker with ice, and shake until chilled. Strain into a tall glass over ice and top with the soda. Garnish with an orange wedge.

Lovage Bitters

1 cup fresh lovage leaves and stems, chopped

1 cup dried lovage leaves

3 tablespoons grated lime zest (use a Microplane)

1 teaspoon celery seed

⅛ teaspoon basil seed

One 1-inch by 2-inch piece lemon peel with white pith

3 cups 190-proof grain alcohol, such as Everclear

2 teaspoons Simple syrup (equal parts water and sugar, heated to dissolve sugar)

2 cups spring water

Combine the fresh and dried lovage, lime zest, celery seeds, basil seeds, lemon peel, and grain alcohol in a clean quart canning jar, wipe the rim and threads clean, place the lid and ring on, and tighten the ring. Store in a cool, dark area with a maximum temperature of 75°F for 2 weeks, shaking the mixture daily to infuse the bitters.

Strain the bitters into a container, add the water and simple syrup, and stir to combine. Transfer the bitters to 1 clean canning jar and wipe the rims and threads clean, place the lids and rings on, tighten the rings, and store the bitters at room temperature. Tightly covered, the bitters will keep for up to 4 months at room temperature.

Sotol Old-Fashioned with Lovage

2 oz. sotol

¼ oz. agave nectar

Tiny pinch of salt

1 dash lovage bitters (recipe directly above)

1 dash citrus bitters (see page 166)

Garnish: orange or lime peel

In a mixing glass filled with ice, combine all ingredients except the garnish, and stir briskly for 20 seconds. Let the drink sit to chill and dilute for 4 to 5 minutes, and strain into an old-fashioned glass with one or two large ice cubes. Garnish with the orange or lime peel expressed over the top.

Sotol Seashore Margarita

2 oz. sotol

¾ oz. lime juice

1 barspoon orange juice

¼ oz. dry vermouth

1 dash citrus bitters (see page 166)

Scant ½ oz. agave nectar

Tiny pinch of salt

Salted rim (optional)

Garnish: orange wedge

Prepare salt rim, if using. Shake ingredients with ice until chilled, and strain into a rocks glass. Garnish with an orange wedge.

Sotol Celery Highball

1½ oz. sotol

½ oz. lime juice

1 oz. celery juice

Tiny pinch of salt

1 dash lovage bitters

Cel-Ray Soda, to top

Garnish: celery tops; lime wedge

Shake all ingredients, except soda and garnish, in a shaker with ice until chilled. Strain into a tall glass and top with soda. Garnish with the celery tops and lime wedge.

TOKEN MEZCAL DRINK

We at Liquid Gold humbly believe mezcal should mostly be drank neat. It varies so much by producer, region, style, and ingredients used in fermentation, it actually deserves its own book. And there are some good ones. Check out *Finding Mezcal* by Ron Cooper, and Robert Simonson's *Mezcal and Tequila Cocktails*. If you love mezcal in cocktails. we recommend subbing it in any of the aforementioned drinks in this chapter; but beware, as mezcal can really take over in a cocktail and throw its stiff elbows around to block many of the subtleties inherent in great cocktails. But if you must, it can be amazing in a super-strong toddy when you've just come in out of the cold.

Mezcal Toddy for the cold nights

1 black tea bag (or tea of your choice)

1½ oz. mezcal

½ oz. agave nectar

1 dash Angostura or cinnamon bitters (page 116)

Tiny pinch of salt

Garnish: orange wedge; rosemary; sage.

Begin by boiling enough water for twice the amount of drinks that you're making. When the water is ready, pour enough into your mug to temper it so it keeps warm for the duration of your drink. Placing a small plate or bowl over the top of the mug can help retain the heat as well. Once the mug is fully hot and ready for action, discard the tempering water and make the tea by pouring more water, adding the tea bag, and covering the mug for maximum extraction.

After 3 to 4 minutes of brew time, set aside the tea bag (for your next hot toddy) and add the mezcal, agave nectar, bitters, and salt. Squeeze a few drops of orange over the top, and garnish with the orange wedge. Rosemary and sage would make for aroma-boosting garnishes as well.

BATS AREN'T ALL BAD

Certain fruit-eating bats are the only known pollinators of the agave plant, which is otherwise dependent on the luck of the wind for reproduction.

SHOTS! IN A BOTTLE

While picking up garbage on the beach in West Mabou, Nova Scotia, Norman Mcdonald (not to be confused with the late comedian) found something peculiar in a 375-ml bottle of Sauza Tequila. Inside was money, and a note explaining that the ashes belonged to a gentleman named Gary Robert Dupuis. Presumably written by a family member, the note went on to explain: "His favorite drink was tequila—straight up . . . If you find him, please take this money, buy yourself and Gary a drink, and release him back in the ocean. My wish is that he gets his dream of seeing the world and finally finds some peace." The note went on to ask those who find the bottle to note their location and return the vessel and Gary's ashes to the sea to continue their journey.

Norman was faithful to the task he had randomly been commissioned for. He took Gary and the bottle to a local dance hall the following Saturday night, placing the bottle on the table so it had a good view. As he watched the dance floor slowly fill up with patrons, he promptly ordered two shots of tequila. After downing the first and staring down the bottle in front of him, Norman realized what he needed to do. He glanced at the folks swaying on the dance floor to see if anyone was watching him. Then he swiftly gulped the other shot for Gary, but this time the tequila burned as it raced down his throat. He added some money back to Gary's drink fund. The very next day, Norman made arrangements with a local fisherman to drop the bottle in deep waters, far from the shore.

FORGET WEED GUMMIES; LOOK TO TEQUILA

Gummies are often the way to go. In an April 2020 *Forbes* online report, Emile Sinclair, cofounder and head of innovation at UK-based Smith & Sinclair, has created a line of tequila-filled cocktail gummies. The "Tequila Time Box" of cocktail gummies, which debuted in the United States, contains ten gummies: two tequila sunrises, two tequila slammers, two palomas, and four spicy margaritas. They have 5 percent alcohol by volume and retail for $25. Sinclair, a chef with classically trained sensibilities, began the gummy project along with his wife as a way to add entertainment to game night with their friends. After selling well at a farmers' market, they decided to give the gummy business a go. During the quarantine, their business grew exponentially, and while they undoubtedly brought out the truth in some family arguments, they also allowed people to enjoy that summer-season tequila buzz just a little bit deeper.

GOATS DRINK . . . TEQUILA?

Michael Jordan, arguably the greatest basketball player to ever live, was thrust back in the spotlight during the strange and tragic early stretch of the pandemic in April 2020. With a nation mostly at home drinking their sorrows, ESPN moved up the start date for their epic longform series "The Last Dance," a ten-hour miniseries all about Michael Jordan and the 1998 Chicago Bulls making one last run for their sixth championship. Even though we all knew how it was going to end, the sheer amount of previously unseen footage, combined with the ever-cocky Jordan sitting down in his beachside pad and throwing out slights to former teammates, enemies, and frenemies alike, was enough to keep many sports fans entertained when there weren't any games to watch.

One of the more peculiar props used in the extensive interview footage was an undoubtedly expensive double old-fashioned glass filled with a dark brown liquor, which most people assumed was whiskey. As Jordan would discuss his career highlights, the glass would appear as if it were emptying quickly, only to be refilled for the next round of questions. One CBS report headline said it all: "The Curious Case of Michael Jordan's Fluctuating Liquor Glass." Whatever it was, it was making him talk, and if the rosy cheeks and eyes reddening like a sun going down meant anything, he was enjoying himself. Booze-sleuths would not be denied, and eventually the truth came out. Jordan was in fact taking pulls off his own ultra-premium tequila label, Cincoro Extra Anejo, which retails for $1,800 and doesn't even come with basketball shoes. Jordan would later tell the *Today Show*, "We decided to do our own tequila. If we sell it, we sell it. If not, at least we got enough to drink." And you wonder why they call him "his Airness."

Thankful for
Thanksgiving

SEVEN

Hot Buttered Fun— Friendsgiving

The cooking ethos of the Julia Child era, "butter makes everything better," is as true for fresh, crackling bread as it is for mashed potatoes.

It's also apt when discussing the finer points of executing kitchen classics, ranging from omelets to pasta dishes to steak and mashed potatoes. Where butter is *under-utilized* is the world of beverage. Butter can be used to "fat-wash" different spirits to give them a luscious mouthfeel in cocktails, and can be creamed (softened at room temperature) to mix different flavors and spices into the butter that you can use in delicious beverages, hot and cold.

Hot Buttered Rum

1 tablespoon butter (cut in half to make two pats of butter)

8 oz. black or herbal tea

1¼ oz. aged rum (try anything El Dorado or Hamilton makes)

½ oz. rich demerara syrup (2 parts turbinado sugar to 1 part water)

2 dashes cinnamon bitters (see page 116)

1 dash apple cider vinegar

Garnish: 1 small lemon wedge

Begin by tempering the mug you'll be drinking out of with hot water. Place a small bowl or plate on top of the mug to seal in the heat. After the mug is piping hot, take off the plate and discard the hot water. Add the butter, hot tea, and all other ingredients except for the lemon, and stir gently for 10 seconds. Squeeze a few drops of lemon juice over the top of the drink, and garnish with the lemon wedge on the side of the mug.

Hot Buttered Pearl Diver

1 tablespoon butter (cut in half to make two pats of butter)

8 oz. black or herbal tea

1¼ oz. aged rum (try anything El Dorado or Hamilton makes)

½ oz. honey syrup

2 drops vanilla extract

2 dashes cinnamon bitters (see page 116)

Garnish: 1 small lime wedge

Begin by tempering the mug you'll be drinking out of with hot water. Place a small bowl or plate on top of the mug to seal in the heat. After the mug is piping hot, take off the plate and discard the hot water. Add the butter, hot tea, and all other ingredients except for the lime, and stir gently for 10 seconds. Squeeze a few drops of lime juice over the top of the drink and garnish with the lime wedge on the side of the mug.

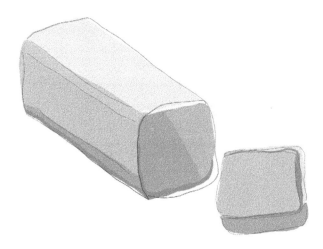

Regular Pearl Diver

Serves 2

- 1 oz. honey syrup
- 4 drops vanilla extract
- 2 tablespoons butter (tempered on the countertop for a few hours to soften)
- 2 oz. aged rum (try anything El Dorado or Hamilton makes)
- 2 oz. Puerto Rican rum (try Ron Barrelito or another gold rum)
- 2 dashes cinnamon bitters (see page 116)
- 1 oz. orange juice
- 1 oz. lime juice
- 12 oz. crushed ice
- Garnish: mint and pineapple fronds

Begin by combining the honey syrup, vanilla extract, and butter in a small bowl and whisking together to combine. In a blender, combine the butter mix and all the other ingredients, except the garnish, and blend on high speed for about 15 seconds. Split into two serving vessels (if you're lucky enough to have a pearl-diver glass, use it!) and garnish with mint and pineapple fronds.

FRIENDSGIVING: BUDGETING FOR YOUR FRIENDSGIVING FEAST

Now let's turn things over to Liquid Gold Cocktail Correspondent and hospitality professional Jessica Backhus about holiday party budgeting and not forgetting the good stuff.

An Adept Guide to Holiday Party Planning

by Jessica Backhus

There are many qualities that transfer easily from the sports industry to the hospitality industry, and vice versa.

One of my favorite books to share with restaurant managers is a coaching book—*Talent and the Secret Life of Teams*—by Terry Pettit, a very successful college volleyball coach. The formulas for success in both arenas are interchangeable and dependent on teamwork, ingenuity, and accountability.

My dad was a great college football coach in his twenties, and many years later was an astute managing partner/owner-operator of a Western-style hospitality venue. He extended his coaching charisma into his banquet and management setting; he used to say he wished he could replay footage from events with the staff—like game footage in the locker room—so that he could revisit how the night went, see who had "dropped the ball," and figure out ways to improve. Now most restaurants have security cameras, and they absolutely can and do turn to footage to keep the guests safe and secure, happy, and—if necessary—accountable in the event of an accident or complaint.

Hosting a holiday gathering is very much like a banquet evening or restaurant service, and relatable to sports when it comes to planning and budgets. Everyone is expected to deliver a satisfying result within reasonable expectations, all while not spending *too much* money. Whether sharing delicious cheer or attempting to win a national championship, working within your means can be challenging but exceedingly successful with ingenuity and creativity.

My dad worked with the great coach Bill Parcells, who was known for innovative success on the football field and in his programs. On Parcells's desk in the football office where a nameplate would normally be, he simply had a sign that read "Runways Last." The coach had taken on the enormous challenge of transforming a losing football team—the Air Force Academy—into a championship team that could, most importantly, beat their rivals at Navy.

When he arrived at the school, he asked the difference between the two institutions. He was told that when Air Force was given the order from Congress to build a new air base, the first thing they would build would be the runways, followed by the airplane hangars, then housing for the officers and enlisted people. Prior to building the Officers' Club, they would run out of money, at which point they would go back to Congress to ask for more money to build the Officers' Club. Congress would turn them down, claiming there was no money left in the budget.

The Navy, on the other hand, when given the charge from Congress to build an air base, would first build the Officers' Club, then the housing for personnel, then the hangars for the aircraft. At this point, they would run out of money and would go back to Congress to ask for the money needed to build the runways. Congress would, of course, appropriate the funds. According to my dad, early in Bill's tenure at the Academy, the weightroom was improved, sweats and workout gear upgraded, uniforms "tweaked," but no new helmets were ordered . . . there was no money left in the budget . . . until there was.

When planning a holiday party, beverages must be at the top of the budget list. Food is necessary, and decorations create cheer, but the drinks you serve at the party are the rug that ties the room together—people would much rather spend time in the Officers' Club than on the runway. Tasty, thoughtful beverages will make the food more delicious, the decorations better appreciated, and will set the tone for the entire night.

A few minor tricks will maximize your funds and efforts and make for a magical evening:

1. Plan ahead—most delicious things take time, so when it comes to beverages and food, put in the early effort to prepare ingredients and let them harmonize. Make teas and cordials and let them steep with herbs and peels, and even seeds—lemon seeds have a lot of pectin, which creates a lovely texture. Slow-cook large-format meats and hearty vegetables—this will go far because many less-expensive proteins benefit from low and slow cooking. Seek out ingredients for the drinks and bites that are in season and abundant in your area; these will be the most delicious and inexpensive resources to utilize.

2. Batch in bulk—make foods in casseroles or loaves that can be cooked on a large scale and sliced or portioned easily for guests

to pick up and eat without a lot of utensils, napkins, etc. If you are ordering from a restaurant or catering company, go for the platters, then stretch them into smaller servings, and plate and garnish them with creativity. Remember that even simple sauces make everything look fancy. Cheese and meat boards are worth cutting and assembling yourself—a block of good cheese and stick of soppressata cost much less and stretch much further if you don't pay for someone else to slice and display them. Distribute an array of chips, dips, and snacky bites in various areas around the gathering—this will distract people throughout the night so the substantial foods will last longer. The order of priority for party food should be sustenance, accessibility, then presentational flair.

When it comes to beverages, create a seasonal specialty cocktail you can make in a large batch—split the batch in two so that some of it remains a non-alcoholic specialty beverage, and booze up the rest with a universally approachable spirit like brandy or vodka distilled from potatoes or corn. Whiskey and tequila drinkers will dive into a delicious and dynamic punch made with a less-expressive spirit, but the same can't be said the other way around. It isn't necessary to offer every brand or style of wine, beer, and spirit under the sun—it is important to make sure that what you offer is appealing and delicious on a universal scale. Versatile, accessible, creative beverage offerings will satiate and delight nearly everyone's palate. Expensive marketing labels needn't dictate the backbone of this drink, and there is massive quality-to-cost ratio to be found in lesser-known spirits. Seek recommendations from a trustworthy sales clerk.

3. Patronize a good local wine-and-spirits shop—you will find better quality recommendations from a wine or liquor store that is independently owned and has knowledgeable staff who will give you honest offerings and will likely give you a discount when buying in bulk. There are incredibly good accessible wines that come from Italy, Spain, Portugal, etc, that will appeal to a broad audience and

cost a fraction of what you'll pay for Buttery Chardonnays and Cali Cabernets. A good shop will also have a selection of sparkling wines in the high-quality, low-budget, mass-appeal category—seek out labels with "Cremant" on them—these are produced in the style of Champagne but come from other areas in France; they are affordable and delicious.

These fine proprietors will also steer you to sippable, delicious spirit diamonds in the rough—whiskey, rum, tequila—that will surprise people but are lesser known and less expensive because they aren't owned by celebrities.

4. Have a stash—and a code word. Wherever you have your bar or beverage cart, keep a couple of bottles of nicer spirits set back for the purists and the people you really want to impress. This can be something you've been saving for a special occasion, or that your trusty shopkeeper pulled out of the back to sell you, or just the gems mentioned above that needn't be on display but round out the offerings so there is something for everyone. These are not the tipples that everyone at the party will appreciate, so they should be distributed by you personally, or put in charge of a bartender who will release their magic only at the prompt of a word or phrase of your choosing—this also makes it more fun and mysterious, and makes people feel special.

5. Utilize your kids (or other people's) to make decorations. Children are creative; and if you give them the tools and a focused task, they will "Buddy the Elf" the room in no time. Colored paper, cardboard, cellophane, even the contents of your recycle bin can make for excellent decorations—if people can drag discarded containers behind a car to celebrate marriage, a holiday party can certainly shine with tin-can wind chimes and aluminum foil awnings.

Holiday parties and celebrations of every kind must have food for sustainability and even for liability, but the drinks will be the star. Next-level beverages crafted with detail and love create a most pleasant ambiance, leave a lasting impression, boost morale, and make for an inspired start to the New Year. The food offerings are the runways of the party—they are necessary to have and to be well made; but, without the people and the merriment and the fun, they are just strips of asphalt. The beverages keep the party going, give the food a purpose, and make the evening memorable. Cocktails first, runways last.

MORE LIQUID GOLD PARTY PLANNING GUIDELINES

+ When seeking out mixers for a punch or batched-out holiday cocktail, dial in your recipe first so you know exactly how much you need. No sense in doling out for a big bottle of Cointreau if you only need a few ounces for your holiday Cosmo. For groups of 6 or 8, often an airplane bottle or 375-ml bottle of some mixers will work just fine and save you money that you can use on sparkling wine. Most 375-ml bottles of vermouth cost around $9.

+ Speaking of the ubiquitous fizzy stuff, look to affordable alternatives to Champagne like Gruet from New Mexico and Segura Viudas Cavas from Spain—one of the most affordable and delicious wines you can buy around the holidays. Segura Viudas retails for around $10 and is very easy to find at most grocery stores.

+ Vinho Verde, the light and mildly fizzy wine from Portugal, is light in alcohol (9 to 10 percent), always very affordable (from $9 to $12), makes a great punch addition, and is versatile with all kinds of different foods. Especially any finger foods that might be set out for hors d'oeuvres like pigs in a blanket or crudités.

+ When batching and/or making punches, don't forget the most affordable ingredient of all: water. Most cocktails we drink in bars, restaurants, and at home have around one ounce of water in them, either from the ice used to shake the cocktail or the dilution from stirring it. If you're planning out a batched cocktail and thinking you'll be serving wine with dinner, use water at your disposal when batching out martinis and Manhattans so you don't get your guests too inebriated before dessert. Plus they'll just taste better and more like they were made to order.

+ Don't forget about "case deals" when it comes to buying wine. If the wine purchasing is split up among three people and they all buy three bottles, buying a case for the same price would potentially make more sense in the bang-for-your-buck department.

Here are some batched cocktail and punch recipes for your friendsgiving revelry:

Party Martini

To a standard 750-ml bottle add:

14 oz. London Dry or Plymouth Gin

6 oz. dry vermouth

3 dashes orange, lemon, or citrus bitters (see page 166)

5 oz. water

2 lemon peels, expressed over the mixture before stirring.

Garnish: olives, lemon peels, any other items that speak to you when it comes to Martinis.

Stir ingredients together (save for the garnish), bottle and cap the mixture, and store in the freezer until it's party time. Serve in 3.5-oz. portions to make 7 martinis. Pour that little extra bit into the glass of whichever friend or relative needs it the most (you know who they are). Garnish the martinis with olives, a lemon peel expressed over the top of the drink and discarded, or some rosemary and thyme you have lying around for the food.

Party Manhattan

To a standard 750-ml bottle add:

14 oz. rye whiskey or bourbon

6 oz. sweet red vermouth

12 dashes of Angostura or other aromatic bitters

5 oz. water

2 pieces of orange peel the size of your finger, peeled very thin with little to no pith, for infusing into the bottle

Garnish: cherries, orange peels, and any other you have around

Stir ingredients together (save for the garnish), bottle and cap the mixture, and store in the freezer until it's time to pour. Serve these in 3.5-oz. portions to make 7 drinks. Once again, that little extra goes to whoever needs it the most! Garnish the Manhattans with cherries and orange peels expressed over the top and discarded.

Friendsgiving Punch

4 oz. bourbon

2 oz. sweet vermouth

1 oz. Cointreau or other orange curacao

2 oz. lemon juice

4 oz. fall-spiced tea (see page 117)

1½ oz. honey syrup (1 part honey to 1 part water)

6 dashes cinnamon bitters (see page 116)

Pinch of salt

1 bottle of sparkling wine

Garnish: dehydrated pear or persimmon slices; thyme

Place all ingredients, except for the sparkling wine and garnish, in a punch bowl, and stir to combine. When it's time to serve, add ice and pour in the bottle of sparkling wine. Stir and garnish.

Booze News FRIENDS AND DRINKING

MY FRIENDS ARE DRUNK, SO I MUST BE

According to the *Smithsonian* magazine—a source for timeless material if there ever was one—a new study has been published by researchers from Cardiff University in which drinkers and club-goers were surveyed based on how drunk they thought they were. Then they were given breathalyzer tests and were asked about how much they had drunk and their long-term health. Nosy much?

What the researchers found surprised them. When surrounded by people who drank in moderation, a person would see themselves as less drunk than the breathalyzer would indicate. Conversely, a person who had only had a handful of drinks might feel more drunk if they were out partying with a rowdy crowd. To the researchers, this helped explain why folks seem to get rowdier when they're hanging out with people who drink a lot. It also spoke to why being around more sober people can have a calming effect on those who might be drinking too much. This also helped explain why having concentrations of bars and nightlife options (cough-cough, downtown Nashville!) leads to a compounding of problems related to large groups of people drinking too much.

"We know that as the number of pubs and clubs increases in an area, you tend to see more alcohol-related harm," said Simon Moore, a coauthor of the study and a professor in public health. "Coupled with our findings, I think we would suggest that altering the mix of venues—that is, bringing more sober people into the night-time environment—might help." Some have suggested hiring ambassadors to come into those areas during high-traffic times and act as designated drivers, and guardians for those who need help. Sounds like this makes way too much sense to ever happen; but great job all around, Cardiff!

MAN HELPS FRIENDS LOOK FOR HIMSELF

In September 2021, *Vice World News* reported that a man who was reported missing by his friends in Turkey accidentally joined his own search party before realizing he'd been the actual target of the search all along. Local media in Turkey reported that Beyhan Mutlu, a fifty-year-old man from a rural region in Turkey, was out drinking with friends when he wandered off into a nearby forest and never returned. When his friends became concerned, they alerted the authorities, who began a search-and-rescue mission to find him. The search began to intensify as more and more neighborhood volunteers joined in the search party. For hours, they yelled out the name "Mutlu," until one of the members of the search party far in the back began to hear what sounded like his name.

In what we imagine to be a deleted scene out of a Will Ferrell movie, Mutlu suddenly cried out, "Who are we looking for?! I am here!" Trust us, this is not merely an existential tale, and it's not the first time it has happened. *Vice* reported on another person declared missing who joined their own search party: in 2012, an Asian tourist who had gone missing in Iceland was later discovered among the search party. Apparently she disagreed with her own description. So much for friends.

WOMAN GETS STOOD UP AT OWN FRIENDSGIVING

In what we'd call a cautionary and sad tale around the holidays, a New Jersey woman was devastated when no one showed up to her friendsgiving celebration. Christian Zamora (Kidalloy on TikTok) shared a video—of his girlfriend, Maryann, sitting alone at a beautifully adorned table when none of her friends showed up—that was viewed nearly 15 million times. In the video, Christian explains how Maryann was planning the event for two weeks, even decorating her entire basement for the soiree. She would later go on to make hundreds of thousands of "friends" on social media.

EIGHT

A Collage of Apéritif— Prelude to a Big Meal

Pablo Picasso gave us all hope in the spring of 2021, at least here in Nashville, Tennessee, as a new exhibit titled *Figures*, complete with seventy-five paintings and sculptures, opened to a completely changed world.

While it was the first major exhibit to grace the art-deco decadence of the Frist Museum since the global pandemic started, it was also the only place to view this collection of career-spanning work in the entire United States. Picasso's mastery of different forms, and his playful exuberance in sidestepping those forms to forge new paths, was a beautiful way to begin to emerge from the pandemic that had changed life as we knew it. It was actually Picasso who introduced me to Suze, the gentian-based apéritif, over ten years ago when I first saw the groundbreaking collage, La bouteille de Suze, or Bottle of Suze, and had to immediately find out what this strange yellow liqueur was all about. Would it give me the same visionary powers as Picasso?

While it appears that Picasso *did* love to sit and read the newspaper for hours and drink Suze (probably with a little ice in a small glass), he was more into absinthe, the drink of the creative class in Paris, where Picasso was spending most of his time in the early twentieth century. As I learned more about these gems of European café-drinking culture, it opened me up to a new way of making drinks. It was a way of throwing things together in a more improvisational (or habitually steadfast) way and using as few tools as possible. The only tool you need is a cheap little "Y" peeler, vegetable or citrus peeler, and you don't need to spend a lot of money on it. Try a few different brands out and see which one fits with everyday ingredients like lemon and orange. The best peelers for citrus will be the ones that can get you as thin a slice as possible, so as not to strip off too much bitter pith. Just watch your fingers.

Picasso Cocktail (White Negroni with Bubbles)

1½ oz. Suze (French gentian liqueur), substitute Salers apéritif if you can't find Suze

1 oz. French dry vermouth

1 oz. gin

Prosecco or soda, to top

Garnish: lemon peel

Combine Suze, vermouth, and gin in a highball or old-fashioned glass over ice. Stir to combine, and top with Prosecco or soda water. Garnish with a lemon peel.

FRENCH CAFÉ SPIRITS
TO USE IN COCKTAILS

PINEAU DE CHARANTES

This regional apéritif of western France has been popping up on cocktail menus in America for the last five years, with increasing frequency. Made from the Charente region's grape juices (usually Ugni blanc and Sauvignon Blanc to name a familiar few) and fortified with unaged Cognac, Pineau de Charantes has a lovely golden color and lively flavor with pleasant acidity. Try it in a spritz cocktail or use it in place of vermouth.

KINAS

The tradition of drinking "quinquinas," or " kinas," was a staple of French café culture throughout the nineteenth and twentieth century. Lillet is one familiar example, though Lillet dropped the "kina" (which translates as "bitter") decades ago and is now a much milder flavor profile. To introduce the bold, refreshing character of the kinas of old, look to Tempus Fugit's Kina L'Aéro d'Or, a faithful reproduction of these former café staples. Think of it like Campari meets Lillet with an herbaceous, citrusy kick that is perfect for a new take on a martini, or over ice with a splash of your favorite soda.

SALERS AND SUZE

Gentian, the botanical which gives bitterness to many of the essential ingredients in the cocktail canon, is something you've probably tasted but didn't realize it. In many cocktail elixirs, from Angostura bitters to Campari and Fernet Branca, gentian is hidden in plain sight. The only way to really experience the pleasant, floral, lemon-meets-dandelion flavor of gentian is by acquiring a bottle of Salers or Suze Gentian aperitif (see the Picasso cocktail on page 218). These bright yellow, mildly bitter palate-cleansers are versatile in many springtime cocktails and go well with lemon, sparkling wine, gin and, you guessed it, tequila.

FRENCH DRY VERMOUTH

The vermouth category is really starting to have a moment, as people are starting to not only use it in an array of new cocktails, but also drink it straight or on the rocks with a twist. If you're interested in diving into the wide world of vermouth, Dolin Dry Vermouth from the Chambery region of France is a great place to start. Loaded with savory and culinary herb tasting notes, Dolin Dry is equally at home in a good martini, spritz or on the rocks with a twist of lemon. It can also give your cooking an herbaceous kick by using it to deglaze pans, and can be added to sauces to boost the flavor.

MAKE YOUR OWN HOLIDAY VERMOUTH

Making your own vermouth at home during the holidays can be a fun way to combine dried and fresh herbs from your garden with some of the random spices in your cabinet that you never use. It's also a fun project for the home bartender because you can tweak it and tailor it to the flavors and aromas you enjoy and the cocktails that you enjoy making with vermouth. Custom negroni anyone? The process starts with an infusion of ingredients into wine (called a maceration). We'll also fortify the wine with additional alcohol to keep the wine stable and draw out more flavor from our botanicals. To source some of these ingredients, check out Mountain Rose Botanicals, who seem to have just about everything.
In a quart mason jar combine the following:

26 oz. dry white wine of your choice

5 oz. vodka

⅓ cup marjoram

⅓ cup dried lemon balm

- 3 fresh lavender sprigs
- 3 rosemary sprigs
- 3 mint sprigs
- 1 tablespoon dried basil
- 2 tablespoons dried wormwood, with flower buds
- 1 teaspoon cloves
- 2 crushed cinnamon sticks
- 2 teaspoons allspice berries
- 2 bags chamomile tea

Keep your jar out of sunlight in a cool, dry place and shake the mixture occasionally to draw out more flavor. After a week add:

- 2 vanilla beans
- 5 sprigs thyme
- 1 tablespoon crushed black cardamom
- 1 tablespoon juniper berries

Let the mixture sit in the same cool, dry area, shaking daily if possible, and after 2 more weeks, strain the mixture through a sieve or cheesecloth. Sweeten to your liking with simple syrup (try adding an ounce of simple syrup at a time until you're happy with the level of dry or sweetness.

ITALIAN GRANDPA DRINKS

When we worked at Holland House, a now-defunct cocktail haven in East Nashville, Liquid Gold cocktail correspondent Jessica Backhus and I shared a love of all things vermouth and amaro. We carried a lot of them and tasted through a whole new world of what seemed like drink soundtracks to abstract European films of the '60s.

We called it the "Italian Grandpa" style of making cocktails: a little bit of this vermouth, a touch of that bitter spirit, some ice, maybe a little soda and an orange peel, and all of a sudden you have something that is complex, light, and delicious. It was named after our co-worker, the dashing Italian black-leather rocker dude named Andréa, who would comment about our European craft cocktail knockoffs—in heavy Italian accent no less—"What da fuck, you guys are making dreenks like my fucking grandfather in Italy, this is a-so weeeird." The best part about making these drinks around the holidays is that it actually makes you salivate for food. I can think of no better way to begin Thanksgiving week than by exploring all the low ABV vermouths, apéritifs, sherries, and fortified wines that can enrich your drinking experience. Picasso, working under his mentor Georges Braque, broke through to a new realm when he created the Suze bottle collage. You can forge new paths in your cocktail game as well, by opening up your bar cart to the second golden age of apéritif.

The Negroni—A Bridge Between the French Café Drinking Style and Bold Italian Flavors

1 oz. gin of your choice

1 oz. Campari

1 oz. French sweet vermouth like Dolin (which seems to go better with gin than many Italian vermouths)

Combine ingedients in a mixing glass full of ice and stir briskly for 20 seconds. Strain into a rocks glass over ice and garnish with an orange peel, expressed over the top of the glass.

For the following, we turn things over to our cocktail correspondent Jessica Backhus out of Charleston, South Carolina.

Autumnal Italian Grandpa Drinks by Geography

by Jessica Backhus

James Bond has inspired many things, cocktails being among the most legendary and longstanding of his legacies.

Though lesser known than the Vesper or old-fashioned, the Americano was the first drink he ordered in *Casino Royale*, and is referred to in many of Bond's adventures. In these references, the Americano's reputation is not as a real cocktail, but more of an alcoholic placeholder to be enjoyed before any real action takes place or *any responsibility is required.*

Rather than evidence of inferiority, I believe this makes it the perfect cocktail. The harmonious balance of refreshing, effervescent, mildly inebriating, appetite-stimulating, and unassumingly pleasant-looking makes it unique among cocktails—it is delightful any time of the day or night, in any situation. In the spirit of progress, learning, and evolution, variations of the original recipe can surprise and delight the palate without complication or convolution and be adapted to any environment for any occasion—the ultimate way to begin the holiday season.

The simple formula combines a balance of bitter and sweet, with bubbles of a sort and the magical oils of a citrus peel, built over ice and jostled or stirred; it is easy to make and to enjoy, and it conjures images of an Italian grandpa sitting on his porch, sipping all day and night with a mysterious smile on his face.

I've compiled variations of the original recipe to honor the nature, elements, and resources of the different regions in the United States as we celebrate the change of the seasons, and prepare for all the holidays of indulgence that we've bundled into the winter months to distract us while we wait for the blooms of spring. I will forever enjoy Italian grandpa drinks as much as or more than any other variety of cocktail; I am thrilled to share my favorite autumnal adaptations, as well as music and movie pairings to accompany them.

Pacific Northwest

1.5 oz. Bonal

Splash of Douglas Fir Brandy, Braulio Alpine Amaro, or both

2 oz. dry alcoholic cider

1 oz. soda water

Lemon peel, expressed and stirred into drink

Garnish: pine or rosemary sprig to fancy it up

→ Listen to "Dry the Rain" by the Beta Band; watch *The Goonies* or *Into the Wild* (or the book it's based on—also a good pairing)

California Wine Country

1¼ oz. Cocchi Americano

¾ oz. Bigallet China China

Dash Regan's Orange Bitters

2 oz. sparkling wine

1 oz. soda water

Garnish: lemon peel, expressed and stirred into drink; citrus-tree leaf to fancy it up

Float of Fernet if you're in SF shaking hands with bartenders

→ Listen to "Tous les garçons et les Filles" by Françoise Hardy or "Non, Je ne regrette rien" by Édith Piaf; watch the movie *French Kiss*

Southwest

1 oz. Dolin Génepy

1 oz. Ancho Reyes Verde

3 oz. tonic water

Garnish: lime peel, expressed and stirred into drink

→ Listen to "This Is How We Walk on the Moon" by José Gonzalez; watch the movie *Welcome to Happiness* or *The Tao of Steve*

Colorado Rockies

1 oz. Braulio Amaro

1 oz. Dolin Génepy

3 oz. soda water

Garnish: lime cheek, squeezed and stirred into drink

→ Listen to "Easy" by the Commodores or "Illegal Smile" by John Prine; watch the movie *Aspen Extreme*

Midwest

___

¾ oz. Nardini Amaro

¾ oz. Cynar Amaro

¾ oz. Carpano Antica vermouth

3 oz. soda water

Garnish: orange peel, expressed and stirred into drink

→ Listen to "Let Him Go on Mama" by John Hartford; watch the movie *Mystery Men* or *Coffee and Cigarettes*

Appalachia

___

1¼ oz. Spanish vermouth or Fino sherry

¾ oz. Cio Ciaro Amaro

2 oz. dry alcoholic cider

1 oz. soda water

Garnish: lemon peel, expressed and stirred into drink; orange wedge and apple slice to fancy it up

→ Listen to "Cornbread" by Dave Matthews; watch the movie *Fantastic Mr. Fox*

Nashville

¾ oz. dry sake, preferably Proper Sake

¾ oz. Cocchi Americano

Splash Suze or Gran Classico

3 oz. soda water

Garnish: (Meyer) lemon peel expressed and stirred into drink; frozen fruit to make it fancy

→ Listen to "Please Come Down" by Adia Victoria or "Bloody Mary Morning" by Willie Nelson

Southeast Coast

1 oz. Punt e Mes vermouth

1 oz. Montenegro Amaro

3 oz. soda water

Garnish: lemon peel, expressed and inserted into drink; red bay leaves to fancy it up

→ Listen to "Natural Mystic" by Bob Marley or "River's Rising" by Leftover Salmon; watch the movie *Peanut Butter Falcon*

Northeast Coast—The Commencement

1 oz. Cynar Amaro

1 oz. St. Germain elderflower liqueur

1 oz. Cocchi Americano

1 dash orange bitters

Pinch sea salt

3 oz. soda water

Garnish: orange peel, expressed and inserted into drink

→ Listen to "Can't Take My Eyes Off of You" by Lauryn Hill; watch the movie *Big Night*

THANKSGIVING WEEK

The "one for you, one for them" ethos—you have to balance turning people on to new things and enjoying the staples they've always loved. Basically, a 50/50 with a touch of Salers for the cool kids, with a stiff martini or old-fashioned for the fussy relatives (you know the one who needs a little extra bourbon kick in that first Manhattan). Introducing some dope absinthe to the brother you haven't seen in a while vs. making Mom a lovely gin and tonic with the rosemary you're using for the turkey.

THANKSGIVING PRE-GAME PUNCH

The older I get, the more I realize that when having friends or family over, one of the most important things to think about—and something I've struggled to think about ahead of time in between planning, prep lists, multiple runs to the grocery store, etc.—is how much time I'll actually be devoting to hosting, hanging out, and engaging with people, as opposed to making drinks or finishing food. Now I'm trying to have more things done in advance, when the prep becomes more of a meditation and less of a "gotta get this done asap" situation. Even with a simple punch that you can serve right when guests arrive for Thanksgiving, or a batched old-fashioned that'll be on call for pre-game and post-game activities, one thing to start a few days out is the oleo saccharum. You're making it special this year, right? It's just citrus peels and sugar, relax . . .

Lemon and Orange Oleo Saccharum

½ cup lemon peels, washed, scrubbed, and dried

½ cup orange peels, washed, scrubbed, and dried

1 cup sugar

First, wash and scrub your citrus and pat dry. Using a vegetable peeler, remove the rinds from the citrus, leaving behind as much of the white pith as possible. Transfer the citrus peels to a medium mixing bowl, add the sugar, and toss to combine. Gently muddle the mixture to help infuse the ingredients. Cover and refrigerate for 48 hours.

Strain the oleo saccharum through a fine-mesh sieve into a clean pint canning jar and discard the solids. Wipe the rim and threads clean, place the lid and ring on, tighten the ring, and refrigerate. Tightly covered, the oleo saccharum will keep for up to 3 weeks in the refrigerator.

Thanksgiving Punch with Herb Ice Blocks

2 oz. brandy

2 oz. bourbon

2 oz. sweet vermouth

1 oz. oleo saccharum (recipe on previous page)

2 oz. lemon juice

4 oz. apple juice or cider

1½ oz. honey syrup (1 part honey to 1 part water)

6 dashes cinnamon bitters (see page 116)

Pinch of salt

1 bottle of sparkling wine

Garnish: Dehydrated pear or apple slices

Put all ingredients, except for the sparkling wine and garnish, in a punch bowl and stir to combine. When it's time to serve, add ice and pour in the bottle of sparkling wine. Stir and garnish.

For the Herb Ice Blocks, fill a few small Tupperware containers with water (leaving a few inches of room at the top to add your herbs). Add savory herbs like thyme, rosemary, sage, and even ornamental kale with its gorgeous purple and dark-green hues. Put on the lid, and let the ice blocks freeze for 6 hours (or overnight), and allow them to temper on the counter for 30 minutes before using in the punch.

Cider Punch with Cinnamon Ice Mold

4 oz. apple brandy

1 oz. sweet vermouth

1 oz. apple butter

2 oz. lemon juice

4 oz. fall-spiced tea (see page 117), or black tea

1 oz. oleo saccharum

6 dashes cinnamon bitters (see page 116)

Pinch of salt

1 bottle sparkling apple cider

Garnish: dehydrated apple slices and thyme

Put all ingredients, except for the sparkling cider and garnish, in a punch bowl and stir to combine. When it's time to serve, add ice and pour in the bottle of sparkling cider. Stir and garnish.

For the Cinnamon Ice Mold, fill a Tupperware container with water, leaving a few inches at the top. Add 3 to 5 whole cinnamon sticks and some star anise pods, put the lid on and place in the freezer for 6 to 8 hours to freeze. Turn the container over periodically to even out the distribution of spices in the ice blocks.

Amaro Cream Punch

(one for the weirdo bartenders)

4 oz. Amaro Averna

1 oz. sweet vermouth

1 oz. oleo saccharum

1 oz. lemon juice

4 oz. chamomile tea or other mild, floral tea

1½ oz. heavy cream

4 dashes cinnamon bitters (see page 116)

Pinch of salt

12 oz. soda water (something heavily carbonated like topo chico)

Garnish: dehydrated orange or apple slices; rosemary

Place all ingredients, except for the soda and garnish, in a punch bowl and whisk to combine. When it's time to serve, add ice and pour in the soda water. Stir and garnish.

Booze News PUNCH

A WHALE OF A PUNCH INGREDIENT

While the traditional Victorian punch gained popularity in England—later making its way to the colonies—sailors from the British East India Company in the sixteenth and seventeenth centuries were the swashbuckling pioneers who popularized the modern versions of alcoholic punch we enjoy today. Maritime rules allotted ten pints of beer per seafarer per day. On long voyages, these stockpiles of ale would become depleted and the shipmen would have to resort to local spirits, brews, spices, and other ingredients to meet their per-diem criteria.

On journeys lasting from months to years before the return voyages, it was not uncommon to use rums of the Caribbean and the Indian Ocean. In fact, Rack Punch, as they called it, is a direct reference to Batavia Arrack, a funky pungent rum indigenous to the port city of Batavia, now known as Jakarta, the capital of what is modern Indonesia. Other than a hefty amount of booze, the other ingredients were loosely based and would vary as often as the sea would allow. Citrus of Asia would add acidity and nourishment against scurvy. The spices of India and the Middle East provided a tantalizing complexity. It was in these conditions that sailors would introduce the waxy and misunderstood substance called ambergris.

Some of the earliest accounts of these punches involved emulsifying a wee bit of whale excrement. Ambergris is created by certain types of sperm whale, who, upon dining on squid, would often have a natural intestinal blockage due to the hardened beaks of particularly large squid. Emitting a fair amount of fat mucus in their intestinal tract, lubricating the way, ambergris would start out as a lump of excrement left to begin its journey to the dinner table, the finest perfume bottles, and the trophy cases of many. There is an entire chapter of Herman Melville's *Moby Dick* devoted to this phenomenon. Hardened and cured by sunlight, salt water, and oxidation, this truffle of the sea is sought after to this day. Even in the sunset of commercial whaling, ambergris is still used by many perfume companies including Chanel No. 5, Givenchy Amarige, and Gucci as an aromatic stabilizer.

Booze News MAKING YOUR OWN SPIRITS

Distilling spirits at home is illegal, for much the same reasons that the federal government asks that you not produce methamphetamine in your basement: you can kill yourself and others around you. I get it, stick it to the man. Americans don't like being told what to do, it's tradition! Perhaps it's done for thrifty reasons. A decent home still can be fashioned for under $1000 and mashing supplies are relatively cheap, an investment that can provide one's family and friends with enough swill to party in the driveway for a long damn time. But a lot of people don't understand how dangerous it is.

In July 2011, in the Boston neighborhood of Lincolnshire, UK, five men were killed instantly and another sustained burns on 75 percent of his body, operating a semi-industrial operation in an abandoned warehouse. Granted, this was a huge operation; but the more alcohol you produce, the more risk you run. Robbing a bank is probably safer. At least if someone comes in smoking a cigar while you're robbing a bank, the whole place doesn't blow up. Unless you are a scientist, leave the distilling to the professionals.

NINE

Wine Pairings Beyond Thanksgiving Turkey

Though there are plenty of things to disagree on when the family gets together for Thanksgiving, one component of the yearly feast of comfort food is without negotiation: you need wine.

Deciding which wines work well at the Thanksgiving table is all about versatility and having a wide variety of styles at your fingertips. Light, fresh, and fizzy might work for those looking for a white meat, skip-the-carbs experience, while those who indulge in second helpings of casserole and mashed potatoes (raises hand) might want two wines in front of them: a luscious red to go with the silky texture of some of the food, and a light pink rosé to balance the contrast between dark meat from the leg and white meat from the breast, ladled with extra gravy. Every year on *Liquid Gold*, we go through different pairings for the various side items common at the Thanksgiving table. By breaking down the meal, you're able to see how much richness is often on the table and look at different wines that cut through the unctuousness, and others that complement these familiar textures. What follows are pairing ideas for every course.

THE ARRIVAL: SNACKING ON APPETIZERS

+ Light-alcohol sparkling rosé like Tintero's Frizzante Rosé.

+ Vinho Verde from Portugal, light and slightly effervescent.

+ Affordable Champagne-esque French sparklers like Cremant de Limeoux's.

+ Certain Kombuchas, like Marin's Apple Juniper Kombucha, would be a great non-alcoholic option to pair with throughout the meal.

+ Vermouth on the rocks—Lustau's nutty, flavorful vermouths would make a nice choice—with a splash of soda and a slice of orange get the palate salivating and ready for a big meal.

MASHED POTATOES: MIMICKING THE BUTTER

+ Here's where you can justify throwing in a crowd-pleasing rich Chardonnay that is sure to please moms and grandmas alike. Nicolette Anctil, a sommelier based in Washington, DC, calls this category "Cougar Juice." French Chardonnays are known to have lighter and more acidic qualities due to their aging in stainless steel, but reaching for an oaked California Chardonnay like Stag's Leap would be a great choice with mashed potatoes. Eden Road out of Australia also makes affordable California-style buttery Chardonnay.

+ For a lighter option, try a Spanish Albariño, like Burgan's Albariño that has a mildly creamy texture and a nuanced minerality to round out the gut bomb of creamy potatoes.

BRUSSELS SPROUTS

+ Since bacon is likely to be a key component to this dish, look to low ABV ciders to both contrast the savory elements of this dish and complement the bacon and funky brassica flavors of brussels sprouts.

+ Gruner Veltliner has a bright, refreshing, vegetal, and peppery quality that pairs beautifully with funky cheeses and brussels sprouts. Brüger is one that finds its way on my table every holiday season.

GREEN BEAN CASSEROLE

+ Another holiday staple and also a great pairing with the vegetal-friendly Gruner Veltliner is the test-kitchen classic, Green Bean Casserole, originally devised by Dorcas Reilly from Campbell's Soup as a vehicle for selling more cream of mushroom soup.

+ Pinot blanc, most notably from the Burgundy region of France, is the white mutation of the pinot gris grape, which is also a mutation of pinot noir. Its versatile quality would be a nice counterpoint to green bean casserole. The German wines made with pinot blanc—known as Weissburgunder, which translates to "white burgundian"—have a pleasant acidity but can differ according to region.

Look for Weissburgunders from the Baden region as a wild card for your Thanksgiving wine spread.

THE TURKEY

+ Before we talk turkey pairings, we'll note that if you forgot to brine your turkey, you can always rub mayonnaise and a little mustard all over the turkey before roasting. As long as you season the turkey well with salt and pepper *after* rubbing the mayonnaise and mustard on the turkey (so that the seasoning attaches to the mayo/mustard), you will have a lovely moist turkey and your relatives won't even realize you forgot this crucial step.

+ Gamay is a wine-pairing chameleon because it works well with so many different proteins, and is delicate enough to pair with lighter dishes as well. It's also great with turkey and will have enough broad appeal to please many different palates. Beaujolais, made just south of Burgundy in France, is a well-known wine for the holidays made with gamay grapes that goes well with both white and dark meat. Its tart sensibilities will sidle up nicely to the cranberry sauce as well.

+ Merlot, while still recovering from its "bad rap" status after being taken down in the movie *Sideways* (*"I'm not drinking Merlot!"* declares the protagonist), is another crowd-pleasing variety due to its velvety tannins. Look for a lighter, accessible young Merlot like Barnard Griffin from the Columbia Valley in Washington.

+ For the advanced crew of wine aficionados, throw them a curveball like an off-dry Riesling or a sparkling Lambrusco, two different but equally engaging wines that will inspire conversation and contrast the rich flavors nicely. Sometimes you might want the conversation to drift to wine, away from politics.

GLAZED CARROTS

+ While not necessarily a staple on everyone's table, glazed and roasted carrots are a big part of my family spread, while the carrot soufflé comes into play closer to Christmas. Skin contact wines— or orange-hued wines—which have risen in popularity over the last five years, can be a great pairing option for everything from mashed potatoes to the turkey. They'd be especially delicious with a mouthful of carrots, and won't linger on your tongue like heavier wines, helping you avoid palate fatigue throughout the afternoon/evening. Metamorphika, from the Catalan region of Spain, would be a lovely choice to pair with any carrot-related dish, and is versatile enough to stand up to other flavors through-out the meal.

+ You may well have a beer-lover at the table for Thanksgiving this year, and this is a perfect dish to think about pairing with beer. Amber ales, even those Oktoberfest beers still sitting in your refrig-erator, can be delicious choices to pair with carrots.

+ Uh-oh. Did somebody just casually plop open the bottle of bourbon? A little whiskey can go a long way when pairing with a diverse feast, and the savory flavor of roasted carrots pairs beauti-fully with a well-aged bourbon. Though one of the definitive foods to pair with bourbon is:

SWEET POTATO CASSEROLE: A DESSERT MASQUERADING AS A VEGETABLE SIDE

+ Is the conversation going off the rails? Or is it just too quiet and awkward as the Fox News father-in-law casts some side-eye at the Anderson Cooper–loving cousin? It may be time to pour a little whiskey to break the ice. And bourbon is a phenomenal pairing for the classic sweet-potatoes-and-marshmallow casserole that we all mock but end up praising by the end of the meal. Look for something lighter than 100 proof with plenty of nuance, like Old Medley 12 year or Makers 46.

+ Savory whites like Muscadet (not muscat) produced from the Melon de Bourgogne grape often have a note of salinity to them that would hold up well to sweet potatoes.

+ Etna Bianco from Sicily is an Italian white wine with a similar saline quality to Muscadet, picked up by the sea breeze blowing in from the Mediterranean. This wine's elegant acidity would contrast nicely with the other rich flavors on the table as well.

+ Sweeter wines like Moscato, or dialing back the sweetness a little to an off-dry Riesling, would go the other route and serve to mimic the sweetness inherent in this dish—and may please any relatives who enjoy sweet wines.

CRANBERRY SAUCE: UNNECESSARY FOR THE TABLE, ESSENTIAL FOR LEFTOVERS

+ Cranberry sauce is one of those Thanksgiving staples that you only have a few bites of, but you're happy to see its bright red color lighting up the otherwise beige components of the yearly feast.

+ What makes cranberry sauce absolutely essential to the Thanksgiving experience is its place in the immortal "Leftover Sandwich," a piled-high monstrosity of leftover turkey, a few brussels sprouts, a spoon or so of stuffing and the enticing combination of cranberry sauce and mayo to even out the ratio of dry ingredients to wet.

+ One year I tried to get way ahead of my Thanksgiving prep and actually made the cranberry sauce ten days ahead to see how the flavor would change. It was a revelation, as the citrus became fully integrated into the dish and made for a satisfying pop of acid on the plate to help counteract all the richness.

+ If you're just pairing cranberries with wine, try a sparkling rosé from the Loire Valley, a region known for aromatic, pleasantly fruity and mineral-driven rosé's that cleanse the palate and go with everything from fried chicken to salmon. Some of my favorites are from Grenelle and Bréze. We're even going to use some rosé wine in the cranberry recipe.

Make-Ahead Rosé Cranberry Sauce

(can be made as far as 2 weeks in advance)

1 package fresh cranberries (12 ounces or about 3 cups)

1 navel orange, thoroughly washed

1 meyer lemon, thoroughly washed

2 sprigs rosemary

1 bundled bunch of thyme sprigs

1 cup sugar

½ cup rosé wine (something light and dry)

Garnish: mint

Wash the cranberries and citrus. In a pot, add the cranberries, sugar, wine, and herbs and bring to medium-high heat, stirring lightly to incorporate the sugar but not to break up the herbs, which you'll be removing later. As the cranberries come to a hard simmer, turn down the heat and allow them to simmer over medium heat for 15 minutes. Remove from heat and zest the entire orange and lemon into the cranberries. Once zested, juice the citrus into a separate cup, then strain the juice through a tea strainer into the cranberries. Stir to incorporate. Remove the herbs and transfer to a container with a tight-fitting lid. Store in the refrigerator until Thanksgiving Day.

Now let's hear from Cocktail Correspondent and Wine-Pairing Savant Jessica Backhus, who has her own unique Thanksgiving traditions.

Traditions, Treats, and Tipples

by Jessica Backhus

People love thanksgiving. It is largely the favorite holiday amongst adults and surprisingly many children, despite the lack of tangible gifts and minimal days off work and school. Why?

Food, drinks, and memories! It is an entire holiday dedicated to the appreciation of eating together, communal gathering, and laid-back social interaction. Just like people go all out with decorations for Christmas and Independence Day, if you have an elevated appreciation for food and drink, Thanksgiving is the holiday where splurging means every bit of your day will be more delicious and instantly gratifying. Even when nostalgia and tradition decree the table offerings stay the same year after year, with luck the quality improves as we aspire to improve our recipes, fancy our presentation, and choose which enigmatic and eager-to-potluck friends we invite.

It's our nature, as humans and Americans want to "up the game" and make every year the most epic celebration ever. The best part of a Thanksgiving feast is that you can hold on to your traditions and still make it all exciting, surprising, refreshing, and memorable.

This is especially true of the beverages you enjoy with your holiday spread. Drinks deserve as much consideration as food and will consume much less time for preparation and execution. And they will complete the experience without adding any burden to your big day. The opportunity for adventure and holiday enlightenment lies within the liquid.

Some of the most unassuming and pleasantly surprising drinks to pair with Thanksgiving foods come from humble beginnings that pre-date the American tradition of enjoying, then exploiting, the wisdom, talents, and generosity of gracious people willing to welcome and share. Raising a glass of anything pleasant will always make for a grand celebration, but something that connects us to stories and traditions allows us to reconcile with the origins of the holiday and honor the spirit of communing, learning, and sharing.

It is a bit confounding how easy it is to rattle off a handful of foods that you associate with a Thanksgiving feast, but often the only beverage that comes to mind is "white wine"—not even a specific type or varietal; that's like answering the question "What do you drive?" by saying "a car." The truth is that it is appropriate and enjoyable to drink pretty much anything on Thanksgiving, because the entire day is dedicated to indulgence. If I can perpetuate the stereotype with a little flair and focus,

I'll tout some of the most delicious white wines to share and enjoy with a variety of foods and a plethora of palates. Cool climates often grow grapes that make for high-acid wines, which tantalize the taste buds, flow with flavors long beyond the swallow, and pair perfectly with most everything you just counted on your fingers, assuming your turkey and taters come out right. Two of my favorite grapes in this category are Chenin Blanc and Riesling. Both have an abundance of exciting aromatics and a beautiful balance of textured fruit and acid, which makes them accessible to a wide range of palates. They also have complexity for days, which makes them an easy topic during awkward pauses in conversation.

I will try Chenin Blanc from anywhere in the world, but my heart is in the Loire Valley with this one. There are many expressions from the rich, almost sweet fruit of Vouvray to the bone-dry and mysterious Savennieres; they range in price from everyday drinking to super-special occasion, and they are all worthy of your attention at the Thanksgiving table. As an extra treat, if you can find sparkling wine (Cremant) made from Chenin Blanc, it is a perfect way to begin or end a celebration.

Riesling is delicious from so many different places and is a perfect gateway wine to discover many unknown and underappreciated Riesling-adjacent grapes in their respective geographies. Try a Riesling from Alsace, France—an amazing area snuggled up with a huge mountain range (Vosges)—and if it delights and surprises you, explore the region's other noble grapes: Gewürztraminer, Pinot Gris, and Muscat, as well as Pinot Blanc, Chardonnay's edgy cousin. These wines deliver cool, fun, perplexing flavors, textures, and combinations. It's like licking snozzberry wallpaper.

For my festivities this year, I choose to bring the story full circle with Riesling from my home state of Colorado. Not only are there grapes growing in Colorado in vineyards up to 6,000 feet of elevation, there are exquisite wines being made by artful farmers who honor the area, the terroir, and the types of grapes that want to grow there, and let them become what they want to be. These growers and makers put tremendous talent, effort, and wisdom into creating something delicious to enjoy and share. The Storm Cellar Winery makes delicious Riesling of a quality and complexity that rivals any in the world. It is a great pairing for fall foods, a people-pleasing sipper with delightful complexity, and a great introduction to a wine region unknown to most of the world.

Another noble beverage with longstanding roots and a largely unknown splendor is mead. Our mead episode for Liquid Gold was unexpectedly one of our most popular, bringing many "mead-heads" out from their forest dwellings. Maybe the oldest alcoholic beverage, it is also one of the most natural, mystical, versatile choices for holiday sipping, or for pairing with a big ol' turkey leg. Brewed from honey (save the bees!), mead is a wunderkind middle ground harmonizing the worlds of wine and beer in a beautifully boozy way. Well-made mead is surprisingly dry on the palate, while elegantly and abundantly showcasing the flavors and aromatics of a bee's hard work and broad range. It's also very sneaky, because all that sugar that gets fermented makes for a deceptively high alcohol content; treat it as you would a big old Cabernet or a barrel-aged stout. Honeytree Meadery offers a gentle and exquisite introduction to mead, with tasty offerings for every tongue.

One of the best things about the season of Thanksgiving is the colors and flavors of all the bounty that nature provides. A lovely and tasty non-alcoholic beverage for giving thanks is apple cider. In most places I've lived, there are farmers making and selling cider that I've been delighted to find hiding in plain sight at the grocery store. This taste of autumn is lovely on its own, enjoyed hot or cold. I love to fancy it up with some warming spices—I dry-toast whole cinnamon sticks, allspice, cloves, etc., in a saucepot, then add the cider and steep it on low heat for up to an hour. Let it cool and sit with the spices overnight in the fridge before straining it. I love to share it hot, cold, even over ice with a little lemon, soda, and aromatic bitters. Not only is it delicious, but it makes your house smell like heaven.

No matter how simple or fancy you want your celebration to be, enjoying the bounty of nature with friends and honoring the angels who harness and transform it into succulent morsels and toastable tipples, means it will be the most perfect, epic Thanksgiving yet. Until next year . . .

Booze News **WINE**

WINE ON MARS—LEAVE IT TO THE GEORGIANS

Although they are very different sciences—space exploration and sustainability—they are intertwined because they are both technologies we need *now*! You know, just in case sustainability doesn't work out and we need to start growing grapes for our wine on Mars.

Agave grows where few go. It requires roughly one-third the water required to produce sugar cane, and about half that of corn. It grows in an arid environment producing nectar that is higher on the caloric index than either as far as investment versus reward. But we don't eat agave, we drink it. In North Queensland, Australia, the MSF Sugar Co. grows agave specifically as a biofuel. Requiring little to no irrigation, nor environmental manipulation like fertilizers, the agave thrives in otherwise abandoned tracts of land. This is extremely good news, considering we all live in questionable times as far as fighting climate change and seeking energy-efficient biofuels for survival. Or maybe we just need to buy ourselves more time to figure it all out.

I know if the human race does survive these troubling environmental times, we will still have to leave this planet to colonize elsewhere, eventually. Luckily, on the other end of the scientific spectrum, there are technologies devoted to understanding life on other planets, and they are in search of other worlds to inhabit all the time. While corporate interests begin to take ownership of interplanetary property, they also try to do their part to slow climate change while seeking a planetary contingency plan. It can seem counterintuitive at times, this futurist Noah's ark.

The Republic of Georgia, a biodiverse country and considered the homeland of grape vinification, is home to the oldest known artifacts and tools of wine production. They're also now on the forefront of space exploration and cultivation. While cultivating over 500 known varieties of grapes for consumption and wine production, a collective of entrepreneurs and scientists engineered the "9 Millennium Project," a study on vertical farming of various grape varieties to test their adaptability to space cultivation. Following the cultivation of certain vegetables by NASA aboard the International Space Station, and the production of potatoes by the International Potato Council in Peru, who successfully grew spuds in a Mars-mimicked environment, Georgia seeks to achieve the same success with grapes. They won't quit until they find a varietal that can withstand the stressful growing conditions and high radiation on the surface of Mars.

WINE ON THE MOON

The first beverage consumed on the moon was wine, sipped by Buzz Aldrin minutes after the Apollo 11 moon landing. But this was no celebratory popping of Champagne. It was merely religious ritual for Aldrin, who was an elder at his church, Webster Presbyterian in Texas. Due to the crew having to wait hours to exit their ship and take those fateful first steps, Aldrin took the opportunity to take communion with the bread and wine he had brought along for that very purpose. He drank his wine from a silver chalice given to him by the church, and spoke to the ground crew back on Earth, saying, "I would like to invite each person listening in, wherever and whomever he may be, to contemplate for a moment the events of the past few hours and to give thanks in his own individual way." He later noted that due to the "one-sixth gravity of the Moon, the wine curled slowly and gracefully up the side of the cup." According to the History Channel, Lunar Communion Sunday is still celebrated annually at Webster Presbyterian to commemorate the interstellar milestone.

THE DRUNK TANKER

In the early evening of May 5, 2020, on a northbound stretch of highway CA-99, the driver of a Cherokee Freight Lines truck hauling wine encountered an oddity. Gabriel Moreno was driving erratically alongside the rig in his sedan, frantically motioning for the truck to pull over.

Fearing a mechanical issue, the driver pulled the rig to a stop on the right shoulder. Mr. Moreno did the same in front of the tanker truck. Dressed in dark cotton boxer shorts, a T-shirt, and a surgical mask, our hero exited his sedan and jogged around the front of the rig toward the passenger side of the cabin, out of the driver's sight. Suspecting hijinks, the trucker pulled the tanker back onto the highway. Out of the driver's view (later revealed on security camera), Moreno climbed up a ladder toward the back of the cargo, abandoning his vehicle, and wiggled loose a release valve, liberating thousands of pounds of pressure and spilling a total of a thousand gallons of red wine on the Golden State Highway as the truck hit interstate speeds. Nearly a mile down the road, a weight gauge on the trailer alerted the driver that his load was lightening. Again, he pulled the freighter to the shoulder, called CHP, and exited the cabin to inspect.

At this point, our hero had positioned himself on the ground, directly under the spill. Flailing about like a child, Mr. Moreno let the wine wash over him, even drinking some of it. The trucker described the actions as reminiscent of a child making a snow angel, only with wine. When the driver protested these actions, Moreno fled on foot, heading south-bound in the direction of his vehicle and was soon apprehended by law enforcement. Multiple reports of the incident by passersby described a half-naked man covered in blood, walking opposite traffic.

Of course, the "blood" witnesses spoke of was delicious, unaged red wine. Though Mr. Moreno did not end up spending much time in jail, immediately after his release he began complaining that he had not been given his square meal. The hero then attempted auto theft within blocks of the police precinct, inside an hour of his release. In his mind, he would be able to get a sandwich, though there is no credible evidence that he ever did. But since his auto theft still qualified under the state-mandated zero tolerance, zero-bail public health ordinance related to the pandemic, he walked again. Twice arrested and twice released, all within forty-eight hours. Sounds very 2020 to us . . .

BENEDICTION BY FIRE: AFTER-DINNER AND DESSERT COCKTAILS

Typically, during the holidays no less, you don't want to hear the words "Mom's got the 151, watch out, shit's about to go up in flames," uttered by your bewildered brother who's glancing at you with a devilish grin as you watch the first flames lighting up in his eyeballs. This, however, was how cherries jubilee came to be one of our family traditions during the holiday season. Cherries jubilee, a relic of the midcentury hotel dining that was central to my mother's holiday memories, is a simple way to add a little show to your table during the festive season.

Cherries Jubilee Cocktail

Serves 4 to 6

½ cup water

½ cup orange juice

1 lb. Bing cherries or any dark cherries, rinsed and pitted

6 oz. bourbon

3 oz. French dry vermouth

1 oz. Kirschwasser (Clear Creek makes a great one)

1 oz. Benedictine

4–6 bowls with vanilla ice cream, for serving

In a saucepan, combine the water, orange juice, and cherries and bring to a boil. Once boiling, turn the heat down to a simmer and cook for 15 minutes. Add all the booze and gently light it on fire with a long lighter (experienced cooks only!). Shake the pan and mix the ingredients together as the flame turns blue. Remove from heat and, using a ladle, spoon the cherry and booze mixture onto the ice cream. Don't set the house on fire!

Bananas Foster Cocktail

Serves 4 to 6

6 tablespoons butter

½ cup brown sugar

1 teaspoon vanilla extract

1 teaspoon ground cinnamon

6 oz. aged rum

2 oz. Guava falernum (see page 129) or Taylor's Velvet Falernum

½ oz. Nocino (see page 60) or Nux Alpina Nocino, substitute ¼ cup walnuts for a less boozy and nuttier version

4 bananas, split crossways and then cut in half

4–6 bowls with vanilla ice cream

In a skillet, melt the butter over medium-low heat, swirling the pan to even it out and not overheat. Add the sugar, vanilla extract, and cinnamon and stir to incorporate. Add the rum, falernum, and nocino or walnuts and turn up the heat to a simmer. After simmering for five minutes, add the bananas and light the mixture with a match, removing your hand quickly so as not to burn it! Allow the flame to caramelize the sugars for a minute, then remove from heat. Pour over ice cream and serve with a spoon.

Booze News HOLIDAY FIRES AND FLAMBÉS

DINERS PLAY UNEXPECTED ROLE IN FLAMBÉ DISH, PROMPTLY SUE

In November of 2013, when the restaurant boom was in full bloom in New York City, plaintiffs Judith Katz and daughter Laura Katz were out on the town enjoying a meal at the packed, buzzy restaurant Bocca East on the Upper East side of Manhattan. After a tableside flambé dish spread its wings of flame a little too far, the mother and daughter found themselves "dowsed in flames, lit on fire, engulfed in flames and severely burned by . . . employees who were in the process of flam-beeing a dish in the crowded dining room." It's unclear who ordered what—and what the "what" even was, as no one seems to know which dish the restaurant was even flambéing in the first place (or they shame-fully won't admit it because they probably shouldn't have been frying wontons in tableside rum firepots!). We have no inside information, that's just our educated guess.

The story, and ensuing court case, are a good lesson in the dangers of fire. Be careful out there, intrepid fire-seeking beverage enthusiasts. The suit sought damages for the injuries sustained by the mother and daugh-ter, described as "fright, shock, emotional distress and wanton disregard for the life, health and safety of others." In 2016, the *Gothamist* noted that there was an alternate public record of the fracas. A Yelp user was created that night, as someone felt compelled to join the service and share their experience of the mother/daughter flare-up. "This is the worst place in the world!!!!! The food is horrible. The service is terrible. I watched someone's hair catch on fire. An ambulance came to take them away. It was due to negligence on their part. I personally signed up for Yelp today just to be able to tell other people not to ever go." And now we have come to the realization: Yelpers are the spawn of every restaurant's tiny little mistakes, angry fish bumping into themselves in the fishbowl . . . er, wait, you don't think setting someone on fire is a tiny mistake? That's the point . . . Be careful out there—all it takes is a tiny mistake when you're cooking with fire. Be sure to have an extinguisher nearby, friends.

CHRISTMAS TREES AREN'T THE ONLY THINGS CAUSING FIRES

According to a report filed by the National Fire Protection Association, fires caused by holiday decorations, excluding Christmas trees, resulted in an average annual rate of one death, twenty-six fire-related injuries, and $13 million in property damage. The report went on to describe how more than two of every five decoration fires happen because decorations are placed too close to a heat source. The most common cause of holiday fires are candles. According to the California Department of Forestry and Fire Protection, December is the peak month for candle fires, with Christmas being the most frequent day they occur. During a four-year study, candles contributed to more than a third of home decoration fires, ninety deaths, 670 injuries, and $291 million in property damage. The *Sacramento Bee* reported on ways to keep your home safe during the holidays, including: make sure to use indoor lights indoors and outdoor lights outdoors; fix any broken bulbs every year you get your lights out; blow out candles before bed; and provide large ashtrays for smokers. Also, maybe keep the 151-proof rum on a higher shelf.

Christmas trees also contribute to fires during the holiday season. In the same four-year study, Christmas trees started an average of 160 home fires in the United States, leading to an average of two deaths, twelve injuries, and $10 million in property damage. Most Christmas tree fires are due to electrical or lighting equipment issues. In a fifth of the Christmas tree fires, a heat source (candle or lighting equipment) was too close to the tree itself. The National Fire Protection Association recommends keeping trees at least three feet away from any heat source, including fireplaces, radiators, candles, heat vents, or lights. And even though you may have seen it done in some old, heartwarming Christmas movie, never use candles to light up the tree.

2020 SUMMED UP IN ONE "FIRENADO"

In what later became one of the most-used drink names in California, the National Weather Service issued a warning for a fire-induced tornado, or "firenado," in the state in August 2020. NWS officials called the event a "once in a lifetime" occurrence, stating that the storm could contain fiery gusts of wind of up to 60 mph. NASA, never one to sit out when crazy shit is going down on Earth, called the storm a "fire-breathing dragon of clouds." Known to weather aficionados as "dancing eddies" of air (yet another drink name!), the worst firenado on record occurred in Japan in 1923. In California, no injuries were reported from the firenado.

HAD TO STOP FOR A COLD ONE

On a hot summer night in July in the town of Bristol Bay, Alabama, local hellraiser Dawson Cody Porter stole a fire engine from the King Salmon Fire Station and drove for fifteen miles with the lights flashing. To break free from the station and set out on his journey, Porter drove the fire truck straight through the closed bay doors, causing $10,000 worth of damage. He was later arrested when he decided to stop at the Fisherman's Bar, a local neighborhood bar. The $100,000 truck was out of commission for weeks as it awaited repairs. Locals reported that Porter's beverage of choice at the Fisherman's Bar was "anything cold."

FOX NEWS SETS OWN CHRISTMAS TREE ON FIRE

Hey, Fox News, you're not the only ones who can create a salacious and entirely false headline to get attention! Okay, so maybe they didn't set the fire, because it's always been burning since the world's been turning, but Fox's fifty-foot-tall Christmas tree, made of metal bars covered in tree branches and decorations, did get set on fire right outside their windows in Manhattan. Fox News hosts predictably flipped the fuck out, using it as an amalgam for how crime was on the rise all over the United States. During his 4 a.m. broadcast the morning after the fire, co-host Todd Piro turned the burn political, declaring, "As some progressives downplay and even deny the existence of a crime crisis, we're seeing it firsthand in New York City, as it shows up on our very own doorstep." The ridiculously opinionated freak went on to say, "This is what happens when you have a lawless city." The suspect, a forty-nine-year-old homeless man, was arrested shortly after the fire and was said to be suffering from mental illness. Do you think that made it into the narrative that Fox seemed so keen on perpetuating? Now, there's honesty. A story on the multiplicity of mental illness in an increasingly fractured American society? Nope, they missed that opportunity, and spent the next few days wallowing in self-pity. After all, that's how some people get through the holidays.

"If he was arrested last night, is he going to be still in jail today? Or will they release him?" said co-host Carley Shimkus, putting the national news focus on one troubled homeless man with a history of mental illness. Co-host Brian Kilmeade jumped in the fray to bemoan, "How soon till this psycho is out again to burn somebody else's tree down, or grab some weapon and harass somebody in the subway? This is emblematic of crime that's hitting in places you'd never expect."

I don't know about you, but I'm never surprised to see stories about bizarre crimes happening in New York City. What I didn't expect was a bunch of Fox News viewers breaking into the United States Capitol. Fox covered that story with a bit more nuance. "Someone did this to spoil our Christmas, but that's not going to happen," seethed co-host Ainsley Earhardt (don't worry, you're not the only one wondering at this point if this is some NFL pre-game show with seven people, and not a news broadcast). "You can't burn us down," she later said. Later in the afternoon as the mug shot of suspect Craig Tamanaha was plastered all over the screen for the day, host Lisa Kennedy Montgomery, on the aptly named show "Outnumbered," had one thing to say: "Fire bug little bastard."

Holidaze

TEN

Eggnog
Is a Riot

Eggnog is one of those traditions that
is so wrapped up in our own warped,
Christmas-movie-distorted brains, mixed
with brazenly red cups at Starbucks
filtered through nostalgia, that we seem
to forget it was also once the drink of
Fourth of July celebrations.

This strange idea of eggnog as a summer drink provides a clue about one of the most important elements of an otherworldly nog: good eggs; and, if you can find it, really good dairy. Eggs are more plentiful during the summer, when the proliferation of bugs keeps the chickens happy and full, which makes the yolks shine like little New Mexican sunsets. This could have been one of the reasons why eggnog was served at family Fourth of July gatherings, or it could be that the country was still young and figuring itself out. How could they have known how amazing Randy Quaid would look crushing little Moose mugs of boozed-up eggnog in his Christmas sweater before he tore through the neighborhood to kidnap his brother-in-law's boss? See what those movies did to us?

As with any beverage containing relatively few ingredients, the quality of the ingredients used in your eggnog is very important. Not to go too far down the portlandian rabbit hole of friends with backyard egg operations, and sourcing from as locally as possible, but you'll notice a huge difference in your nog if you're using the kind of dark orange yolks you see on Netflix cooking shows. Ask around at the markets and get ready to bribe that weird neighbor down the street who you're pretty sure is running a three-hen operation on his half acre. Obsessively inquire at the local farmers' market about any local dairy options that may be available. In Middle Tennessee we're lucky to have access to Hatcher Farms and Cruze Family dairy products—the kind of hormone-free, rich, fresh and sweet milk that lifts a nog to transcendent heights. Come on, you know you've been looking for a way to use that KitchenAid mixer that's still sitting in the pantry or taking up space on your countertop.

Once you've got your eggs sourced and figured out (you bought the good ones, right?), and you finally found a dairy operation where you know the cow's name, what it eats, how many massages it gets a week, it's time to talk about booze. And, as usual, I could go on for hours about it. One of the most important things to think about when it comes to nog booze adjuncts, is that eggnog has a pleasant, ice-cream-like aroma. Even if you add one (or more, no judgment) ounce of alcohol per egg in your recipe—a solid format if there ever was one for nog—it can be difficult to find the right mix of flavorful, complex, comforting, and delicious that is so crucial to nog. Am I reaching my limit for how many times I can say nog in one paragraph? No? Perfect.

To boost the *aroma* of your eggnog, which can enhance the sensory memory perception and basically create new traditions on the spot, sometimes you gotta go with the good stuff. And by "good," I mean romantically aromatic. Give me some cognac that smells like a leather chair, a rum that smells of bananas foster and bad decisions, a bourbon or rye with spice and tobacco firepower. Throw in an allspice liqueur, falernum (remember the nut allergy potential), aromatic bitters of all stripes, and (to borrow a tradition from some international varieties [see page 315 for Canadian Moose Milk recipe]) you can try coffee or espresso liqueurs to boost the flavor. Please enjoy these nog traditions and variations on noggy libations, which include movie pairings for each drink. So many nogs and so many movies, so little time . . .

The Only Eggnog Recipe You Need

12 eggs

1 cup plus 3 tablespoons organic sugar (tan color, divided)

3 pints whole milk

3 cups heavy cream

6 oz. cognac

3 oz. bourbon or rye

3 oz. aged rum (spiced rum is fine, if you must!)

1 oz. allspice liqueur (see page 141) or St. Elizabeth's Allspice Dram

6 teaspoons freshly grated nutmeg

1 vanilla pod, scraped

Separate the eggs; beat the yolks in a stand mixer for a minute or so until they lighten. Gradually add one cup of sugar and keep beating until it dissolves. Add milk, cream, booze, and nutmeg slowly, stirring throughout. Add the vanilla, and whisk to incorporate.

Beat whites in separate bowl until soft white peaks form. With mixer running, slowly add the 3 tablespoons of sugar until the peaks stiffen. Whisk beaten egg whites into mixture and garnish with fresh nutmeg.

Top with aromatic bitters or Peychaud bitters (for the red pop of color) as needed.

→ Paired with *National Lampoon's Christmas Vacation*

Chocolate Eggnog

12 eggs

1 cup plus 3 tablespoons organic sugar (tan color, divided)

3 pints chocolate milk

3 cups heavy cream

6 oz. cognac

3 oz. bourbon

3 oz. aged rum

1 oz. Godiva chocolate liqueur

6 teaspoons freshly grated nutmeg

1 vanilla pod, scraped

Separate the eggs; beat yolks in a stand mixer for a minute or so until they lighten. Gradually add one cup of sugar and keep beating until it dissolves. Add chocolate milk, cream, booze, and nutmeg slowly, stirring throughout. Add the vanilla, and whisk to incorporate.

Beat whites in separate bowl until soft white peaks form. With mixer running, slowly add the 3 tablespoons of sugar until the peaks stiffen. Whisk beaten egg whites into mixture and garnish with fresh nutmeg.

→ Paired with *Die Hard*

Caribbean Eggnog

12 eggs

1 cup plus 3 tablespoons organic sugar (tan color, divided)

3 pints whole milk

3 cups heavy cream

5 oz. Jamaican rum

3 oz. Cruzan white rum

3 oz. Foursquare rum (it's okay to use the good stuff)

1 oz. allspice liqueur (see page 141) or St. Elizabeth's Allspice Dram

1 oz. banana liqueur (try Tempis Fugit Crème de Banana)

6 teaspoons freshly grated nutmeg

2 dashes cinnamon powder

1 vanilla pod, scraped

Separate the eggs; beat yolks in a stand mixer for a minute or so until they lighten. Gradually add one cup of sugar and keep beating until it dissolves. Add milk, cream, booze, and spices slowly, stirring throughout. Add the vanilla, and whisk to incorporate.

Beat whites in separate bowl until soft white peaks form. With mixer running, slowly add the 3 tablespoons of sugar until the peaks stiffen. Whisk beaten egg whites into mixture and garnish with fresh nutmeg.

→ Paired with *Christmas Chronicles 2*

Vegan Eggnog

(Lean on canned coconut milk, similar to sweetened condensed milk in texture, to make this vegan-friendly nog for your vegan guests this year.)

- 2 cups almond milk
- 2 cups coconut milk
- 1 (14 oz.) can full-fat coconut milk
- ⅓ cup maple syrup
- 4 teaspoons freshly ground nutmeg
- 1 dash powdered cinnamon
- 1 teaspoon pure vanilla extract
- 1 small pinch salt
- 2 oz. bourbon
- 2 oz. aged rum

Combine all ingredients except booze in a blender, and blend to incorporate everything. Then slowly add the booze to the mixture and blend on lowest setting, building up to a medium setting. To serve, garnish with nutmeg and an optional dash of aromatic bitters.

→ Paired with *The Family Stone*

Sherry and Red Wine Nog

12 eggs

1 cup plus 3 tablespoons organic sugar (tan color, divided)

3 pints whole milk

3 cups heavy cream

5 oz. Oloroso sherry

3 oz. vodka

4 oz. good red wine, something with body like a Cabernet

1 oz. allspice liqueur (see page 141) or St. Elizabeth's Allspice Dram

6 teaspoons freshly grated nutmeg

Separate the eggs; beat yolks in a stand mixer for a minute or so until they lighten. Gradually add one cup of sugar, and keep beating until it dissolves. Add milk, cream, booze, wine, and spices slowly, stirring throughout.

Beat whites in separate bowl until soft white peaks form. With mixer running, slowly add the 3 tablespoons of sugar until the peaks stiffen. Whisk beaten egg whites into mixture and garnish with fresh nutmeg.

→ Paired with *A Christmas Story*

White Vermouth Nog with Black Lime

(for the Ultimate Black and White Christmas movie)

12 eggs

1 cup plus 3 tablespoons organic sugar (tan color, divided)

3 pints whole milk

3 cups heavy cream

5 oz. Cruzan white rum

5 oz. Carpano Bianco vermouth

3 oz. Manzanilla sherry

1 oz. Cointreau or other orange Curacao

6 teaspoons freshly grated nutmeg

2 teaspoons black lime powder, plus a few teaspoons to use for garnish

Separate the eggs. Beat yolks in a standing mixer for a minute or so until they lighten. Gradually add the one cup of sugar, and keep beating until it dissolves. Add milk, cream, booze, and spices slowly, stirring throughout.

Beat whites in separate bowl until soft white peaks form. With mixer running, slowly add the 3 tablespoons of sugar until the peaks stiffen. Whisk beaten egg whites into mixture and garnish with fresh nutmeg and black lime powder.

→ Paired with *It's a Wonderful Life*

Zombie Eggnog

12 eggs

1 cup plus 3 tablespoons organic sugar (tan color, divided)

3 pints whole milk

3 cups heavy cream

5 oz. Jamaican rum

2 oz. Plantation OFTD Overproof Rum (substitute Wray and Nephew overproof if you can't find OFTD)

3 oz. Foursquare rum (it's okay to use the good stuff)

1 oz. allspice liqueur (see page 141) or St. Elizabeth's Allspice Dram

1 oz. Taylor's Velvet Falernum

1 teaspoon vanilla extract

6 teaspoons freshly grated nutmeg

2 dashes cinnamon powder

Separate the eggs; beat yolks in a stand mixer for a minute or so until they lighten. Gradually add one cup of sugar, and keep beating until it dissolves. Add milk, cream, booze, and spices slowly, stirring throughout. Add the vanilla, and whisk to incorporate.

Beat whites in separate bowl until soft white peaks form. With mixer running, slowly add the 3 tablespoons of sugar until the peaks stiffen. Whisk beaten egg whites into mixture and garnish with fresh nutmeg.

→ Paired with *Bad Santa*

HOST YOUR OWN NOGAPALOOZA PARTY

If you feel like getting real noggy *with it* this holiday season, and lord knows we've been itching to party after the doldrums of the last few years, try throwing together your very own "Nogapalooza" eggnog party, where your friends can create their own batches of eggnog and get creative with the holiday staple. No, this wasn't our wild idea. This dairy-fueled extravaganza was the brainchild of Southern Grist Brewing in Nashville, Tennessee. Known for being wildly creative with their beers—from blueberry cobblers and peanut butter stouts to a "mixed greens" IPA series with forty-five iterations—the people at Southern Grist really know how to party and let loose after a long day of brewing and serving beer to the throngs who visit their taprooms daily. We covered Nogapalooza 2019 on a holiday episode of *Liquid Gold*, where the nogs ranged from spicy with cayenne and ginger flavors to fruity with strawberry and blueberry versions. Though there are few rules when it comes to creating a new-school nog utilizing any number of wild flavor combinations, it does help to have a base from which to build your own unique nog. We'll follow the lead of the master brewers at Southern Grist, who prefer a base with egg yolks, leaving out the whites, which can be saved for that hangover egg-white omelet the following day. Here's one template you can use for a nog base, from which to build more flavor on top of:

Nogapalooza Base

12 egg yolks

1 cup plus 3 tablespoons organic sugar (tan color, divided)

3 cups heavy cream

12 oz. brandy, whiskey, or rum, or a combination of all three

Pinch of salt

6 teaspoons freshly grated nutmeg

Separate the eggs; beat yolks in a stand mixer for a minute or so until they lighten. Gradually add one cup of sugar, and keep beating until it dissolves. Add milk, cream, booze, and nutmeg slowly, stirring throughout. Whisk to incorporate.

After making your base, you can start to think about different flavor combinations. Once I had attended a proper nogapalooza, I had the itch to try a cinnamon-chocolate variety, similar to the flavors of churros, made in eggnog form:

Churro Eggnog

So, to the base I added:

2 oz. chocolate syrup (see page 295) or Hershey's is fine in a pinch

3 cups cinnamon cereal-infused chocolate milk (infuse the chocolate milk with Cinnamon Toast Crunch for an hour, then strain the cereal out).

Combine the syrup and cereal milk and whisk into the base recipe. Enjoy with grated cinnamon over the top.

PRESIDENTIAL EGGNOGS

Presidents, including Dwight Eisenhower and George Washington, are known for their own eggnog recipes, which were published in many newspapers of their respective days. Try out these recipes next time the family starts arguing about politics at Christmas. History won't necessarily change the subject but it will definitely steer it in a different direction.

Dwight D. Eisenhower "Ike" Nog

Known for being proudly adept in the kitchen, Eisenhower often dealt with the stress of being a general, and later a president, by cooking his own meals from time to time. During the holidays, Ike's favorite beverage was eggnog, and this recipe from the Dwight D. Eisenhower presidential library shows his affinity for the little details, like carefully pouring the booze in slowly, and not whipping the batch too aggressively, to achieve a lighter, frothier final product.

12 egg yolks

1 lb. granulated sugar

1 quart bourbon

1 quart coffee cream (we're guessing he means half-and-half, or you can substitute whole milk)

1 quart whipping cream

Put the dozen egg yolks in an electric mixer. Feed in the granulated sugar very slowly, so as to get a completely smooth, clear, light mixture. When this is perfectly smooth, begin to add the bourbon very slowly. (The process up to here would normally consume at least 30 minutes—with a good mixer.) Add the quart of coffee cream.

Put the whole thing in the icebox until a half hour before serving, at which time the whipping cream should be beaten until only moderately thick. Be careful not to get it too thick. Mix it slowly into the mixture and serve with nutmeg.

GEORGE WASHINGTON AND THE CASE FOR AGING NOG

The first and most popular eggnog recipe to be widely circulated throughout the United States was from none other than George Washington, "written in his own hand," as it was denoted at the time, and the first president knew the importance of a good drink. He was said to drink a bottle of Madeira a day (baller), followed by whiskey, rum, and plenty of beer. According to Ted Smith of *Thrillist*, George Washington spent 7 percent of his presidential income on alcohol, and, according to *Modern Drunkard*, his estate was once America's biggest whiskey producer, bottling 11,000 gallons in 1799. The lesson: when water is deemed unsafe and replaced by Madeira and whiskey, you can get more things done. Maybe that's not the lesson, actually.

But there are a few valuable lessons to be learned from Washington's nog recipe. First, he suggests you let the nog age for "several days." Aging eggnog is always a great idea if you have the foresight to think ahead about making a batch days or weeks before you'll be enjoying it. As the nog ages—pasteurized by the booze—the mouthfeel of the drink becomes rich and smooth, the egg taste fades away, and the flavors from the booze begin to meld in a beautiful way. According to a report from *Cooks Illustrated*, in which microbiologists Vince Fischetti and Raymond Schuch from Rockefeller University in New York City added salmonella bacteria to a batch of eggnog, it took three weeks for the alcohol to render the eggnog completely sterile. So, there's your sweet spot if you're ever concerned about bacteria levels in your eggnog. As George Washington notes in his recipe, often "several days" of aging is enough to allow the flavors to meld nicely and give you a nice balance of sweetness, richness, and boozy goodness.

George Washington's Aging Nog recipe, via the Alamanac

1 quart cream

1 quart milk

1 dozen tablespoons sugar

1 pint brandy

½ pint rye whiskey

½ pint Jamaica rum

¼ pint sherry

12 eggs

Mix liquor first, then separate yolks and whites of the eggs, add sugar to beaten yolks, mix well. Add milk and cream, slowly beating. Beat whites of eggs until stiff, and fold slowly into mixture. Let set in cool place for several days. Taste frequently.

Booze News EGGNOG

THE EGGNOG RIOTS OF 1826 (AND THE COMING 200-YEAR ANNIVERSARY PARTY)

If you love the movie *A Few Good Men* and eggnog, you're going to love this story. On the evening of December 22, 1826, a large amount of whiskey was smuggled onto the United States Military Academy base in West Point, New York. The purpose? To fortify a huge batch of eggnog for the young cadets' somewhat secret—and annual—Christmas Eve party. Since the 1820s was a particularly lewd period for the cadets, with a steady increase of gambling, tobacco use, and drinking, the cadets were informed that the 1826 Christmas eggnog would be, to quote the parlance of our times, "zero proof," or alcohol free. Jefferson Davis, who would later go on to become the president of the Confederate States in 1861 (rough timing), was one of ninety cadets—and one of twenty-two to later be court martialed—who said, "fuck that, let's smuggle some whiskey and party."

The night began innocently enough with a party in room 28 involving nine cadets. As the party wore on and word got out, more joined the increasingly louder soiree. Another party sprung up in room 5, before cadet David Farrelly snuck out to acquire another gallon of whiskey early Christmas morning. Later, as singing began to fill room 28, Captain Ethan Allen Hitchcock, who was sleeping in the room below, was awakened from his slumber. He went straight up to the room and found at least six very drunk cadets, and a few who were completely passed out. After shaking the sleeping cadets awake and sending them back to their room, Captain Hitchcock confronted cadet James "Weems" Barrien, who would have none of it. Barrien and Hitchcock engaged in a shouting match, and even as Hitchcock left the room, Barrien continued his rage, inspiring cadet William Murdock to form a mutiny against Captain Hitchcock.

Lieutenant William A. Thornton, who had slept through most of the partying at that point, was awakened in his room and upon entering the hallway was attacked by two cadets. One of the cadets, William Fitzgerald, brandished a weapon and was promptly arrested by Thornton. Fitzgerald escaped Thornton's grip and retreated to room 29, where he found two cadets ready to assist him. As Thornton pursued Fitzgerald, he was distracted by loud noises coming from another room. As he turned down another hallway, cadet Samuel Alexander Roberts promptly knocked out Thornton. Sounds of broken windows rang out, and the faint sound of a gunshot awakened even more officers. By 6:00 Christmas morning, the symphony of chaotic sounds reported by witnesses included more glass breaking and gunfire, cries of pain, profanity and furniture destruction. Basically, a Vin Diesel movie with period military garb. Twenty-two cadets were place under house arrest. On January 6, 1827, a date that would later live in infamy when crazed Trump fans would storm the nation's capital, a court of inquiry was ordered to investigate the Eggnog Riots. If disciplinary action was necessary, cadets and other military personnel were to be court martialed. In the end, eighteen cadets were expelled. Private John Dougan was sentenced to one month of hard labor and was forced to forfeit his whiskey ration during the month. The lesson? Don't take away a soldier's whiskey on Christmas Eve.

WHEN EGGNOG GOES DOWN THE WRONG PIPE

Utah man (start a story with that, and we're in for anything) and apparent nog newbie Ryan Roche was rushed to the hospital after he chugged a quart of eggnog in twelve seconds at an office holiday party. In what seems like a cautionary tale of holiday irony gone wrong, Ryan was just about to leave the party to head back home with his wife and relieve the babysitter watching their three kids, when he decided, "eh, fuck it, I got time for this," and decided to enter the contest last-minute. The thirty-three-year-old man was so good at chugging this eggnog that he shaved a whole ten seconds off the previous record of twenty-two seconds. Roche told ABC News Today, "Everyone knows I'm pretty competitive," and, in what were almost famous last words, he went on: "I just decided I was going to win. So I pretty much opened it up and poured it down my throat." His dominant win gave him the aforementioned office record of twelve seconds and a $50 gift certificate to Ruth's Chris Steak House, which, if experience tells us anything, will only translate to him splurging a little extra on that steak dinner and is thus a win for Ruth's Chris.

"Two hours later, I was laying on the couch, shaking uncontrollably, nauseous, having fevers and panting," said Roche. As a friend rushed him to the hospital, Roche quickly descended into pneumonia due to the eggnog literally going down the wrong pipe. Since this was Utah and the eggnog was alcohol-free (what kind of office party was this, anyway?), he luckily didn't have the extra issues of dealing with too much alcohol at once. It was all nog. Roche spent a full day in the ICU and two more days recuperating at the hospital. "It was not fun," he said. "People are emailing me pictures of eggnog; it never gets old. I'm pretty competitive, but unfortunately, in this situation it got the best of me. It's become quite the story."

ELEVEN

Christmas Traditions at Home and Abroad

When it came to driving out into the stark, dark, snowy Indiana countryside for a Rockwellesque Christmas Eve dinner where even the town preacher was expected to show (and have a beer), the drive back was always the scary part.

Hopped up on holiday revelry with a belly full of ham, potato casserole, and Beth Westfall's homemade whiskey cream, my family—which at the time consisted of my grandparents (both have since passed), my parents, and my brother—would load into a Lincoln Town Car the size of a pontoon boot, with a back seat that had more legroom than first class on a DC-9, and drive into the star-splashed night, contending with often cold and wet Midwestern winter road conditions. I would stare off into the peaceful pale horizons, mesmerized by the blank canvas of Indiana farm country in winter, and try to convince myself that we weren't about to go careening off the road into a ditch. If there happened to be a snowstorm whipping powder at the car from every direction, I'd look at my brother and his sarcastic shoulder-shrugging devilish grin, which telepathically told me, "This could be it, but that was a damn good meal," and I'd white-knuckle the leather-coated armrest until we pulled into the driveway of my grandparents' house. Was it Beth Westfall's homemade whiskey cream that kept our cheeks rosy, or the balmy temperature my grandma kept the thermostat on in December? Who cares? All we knew was this was the only time of year we'd be eventually cold as hell (anytime we even stepped outside to take the garbage out) *and* warmed to the bones with a beguiling mixture of cream, chocolate, coffee, and a fair amount of whiskey. Making your own version of this whiskey cream—and don't be afraid to substitute rum or an extra-aged anejo tequila if you are fond of those spirits—is a touch more time-consuming than sitting and drinking, but the results are definitely worth the wait.

Chocolate Syrup

If you're in a holiday pinch, and we've all been there, where you've got too many things to get done and too many people, gifts, and functions to keep track of, opting for a quick trip to the store for some Hershey's chocolate syrup when making your own whiskey cream (hey, at least you're doing something as badass as that!) is just fine. However, if you want to take your whiskey cream to the next level, or give it out as gifts to all your lucky friends, making your own chocolate syrup can really boost the overall flavor. And it doesn't take but 30 minutes or less to put it all together.

2 cinnamon sticks

4 cloves

1 star anise pod

2 allspice berries

1 cup cocoa powder

1 cup sugar

1 cup water

Pinch of salt

1 teaspoon vanilla extract

Toast spices in a skillet on medium heat until fragrant. In a pot, combine the spices, cocoa powder, sugar, water, and salt, and bring to a boil. Immediately turn down the heat and allow the syrup to simmer with a lid on for 20 minutes. Take off heat and allow the syrup to cool, then add the vanilla extract. Will keep for a month, or longer if you add an ounce of vodka, or other spirit like rum or bourbon.

Whiskey Cream

- 1 cup heavy cream
- 2 teaspoons ground coffee
- 2 tablespoons chocolate syrup
- 1 teaspoon vanilla extract
- Pinch Maldon sea salt (or other flaky sea salt)
- 1 (14oz.) can sweetened condensed milk
- 1½ cups bourbon (or split between aged rye and bourbon)

Add ingredients, except booze, to a blender, and blend on a low setting, leaving a hole in the top of the blender to slowly add the whiskey. Once the booze is added, slowly increase the speed on the blender to incorporate the ingredients.

Whiskey Cream Hot Chocolate

- 1½ oz. whiskey or rum cream
- 5 oz. hot chocolate
- 1 dash aromatic bitters (or Angostura cocoa bitters would be great)
- Garnish: whipped cream; marshmallows

Add the whiskey cream to a warm mug of hot chocolate, and stir to combine. Add the aromatic bitters and stir them in. Garnish with whipped cream or marshmallows.

Rum Cream

This slightly more spiced version of a boozy cream beverage is made with rum and bolstered by more spices.

1 cup heavy cream

2 teaspoons ground coffee

2 tablespoons chocolate syrup

1 dash powdered cinnamon

1 dash allspice

1 teaspoon ground nutmeg

1 teaspoon vanilla extract

Pinch of salt

1 (14 oz.) can sweetened condensed milk

1½ cups aged rum (or split between Jamaican and Puerto Rican)

Add ingredients, except booze, to a blender, and blend on a low setting, leaving a hole in the top of the blender to slowly add the rum mixture. Once the booze is added, slowly increase the speed on the blender to incorporate the ingredients.

THE SHAKEN WAY TO WHIPPED CREAM

Don't make the mistake that so many unaware bartenders have made before you, back before anyone could whip out their phone and consult with YouTube and immediately become an expert. Back in the day (oh shit, did I just say that?), we had to artfully pretend we knew what we were doing, even when we clearly didn't. It was a skill that was part of the job. But to see any bar or establishment that has heavy cream on hand to then run out of whipped cream for a topping, or not even mention that they've got heavy cream on hand is just unnecessary. For beautifully fresh whipped cream to top desserts or drinks with, all you need are some shaker tins and a cup of heavy cream. Simply shake the heavy cream vigorously for about a minute, taking care to keep the seal tight while you shake so you don't have an explosion of cream just as you're trying to finish a drink. The result is an airy, whipped and light delight, perfect for topping everything from eggnog to apple pie to hot chocolate.

TOM AND JERRY

Another Midwestern Christmas classic, great for watching the falling snow, is the Tom and Jerry, like a warm bowl of eggnog . . . wait, that didn't sound right. Just trust us, this drink will please the whole party. This pre-prohibition holiday classic from legendary bartender Jerry Thomas (hence the name) is very similar in preparation to the eggnog recipes above. However, what sets the Tom and Jerry apart is that it is served warm. Since hot and warm drinks can temper easily and lose their warming luster, it's a good idea to serve this drink in pre-warmed mugs or cups (or go to eBay for the authentic Tom and Jerry punch bowl and cups, pictured). The first step in making a Tom and Jerry is putting together the batter that you'll mix with warm milk and booze later.

The Batter

12 eggs

1 oz. aged rum (I like any of Foursquare's delicious rum for something this special)

4 cups organic sugar

½ oz. allspice liqueur (or St. Elizabeth's Allspice Dram)

2 teaspoons freshly ground nutmeg

1 teaspoon powdered cinnamon

1 teaspoon ground cloves

1 teaspoon Maldon sea salt

½ teaspoon ground mace

Separate the eggs; beat yolks in a stand mixer, slowly adding the rum, for a minute or so until they lighten. Gradually add sugar, and keep beating until it dissolves. Add the spices, and beat to incorporate.

In a separate bowl, beat the egg whites until soft peaks form. Gently fold in the egg whites to the yolk/spices/booze mixture. If making ahead, cover and refrigerate until it's Tom and Jerry time. With the booze in this mixture, it will keep for at least a week.

Tom and Jerry Time

9 oz. Tom and Jerry batter (recipe on page 301)

24 to 32 oz. whole milk, hot

6 oz. aged rum

4 oz. cognac

Garnish: grated nutmeg and cinnamon stick

In a heatproof punch bowl combine the batter and hot milk, and slowly add the booze, whisking as you go. Serve in pre-warmed mugs or cups, and garnish with freshly grated nutmeg and a cinnamon stick.

Before we dive into Christmas traditions around the world, let's turn things over to Liquid Gold Potions Master, Brittany Augustine, who takes us to the mystical, faraway land of wizards and witches in the Harry Potter universe. When it comes time for your Harry Potter holiday marathon, you'll have plenty of new cocktail recipes to get you through.

Harry Potter Cocktail Party

By Brittany Augustine, Liquid Gold Potions Master

The fall and winter seasons mean something different for everyone, as the cool air and short days usher in the holidays and the nostalgia that goes along with them.

The excitement and sense of wonderment I had as a child—based on the unknown around the corner—was balanced by the upholding of certain familiar traditions. As I've grown older, I realize that I'm no longer as excited about the anticipation of Christmas morning, but rather the traditions I've made along the way with family, and friends who have become family. When the holidays come around, there are tried and true traditions I look forward to: decorating the tree, my friend's annual Christmas dinner, and most importantly, the annual *Harry Potter* marathon. Yes, *Harry Potter* is in fact a Christmas movie!

One thing that has remained constant over the years is my love for the Harry Potter series. I read the first book when I was eight years old and I am still filled with the same sense of wonder and awe over twenty years later. When the books first came out, there was a lot of discussion regarding whether or not it would be "safe" for kids to read. So, like many other kids at the time, I begged my mom to let me read it. She decided she would read it first to see what all the fuss was about. Well, she fell in love immediately, and passed along that first book to me. From then on, I would stay up until midnight for the book releases and have my dad take me to Walmart with him so I could get my hands on the book before my mom. I would spend the following night and day locked in my room reading. One of my favorite traditions every holiday season is to spend two days with my best friends, watching the entire series while wearing matching themed pajamas and making food and cocktails inspired by the books and movies. Below I've listed some ideas for you to use for your very own wizarding marathons. Whether you're watching these mystical movies for the first time or the millionth, there are plenty of adult beverages to enjoy with them.

BUTTERBEER, TWO WAYS

Even muggles and squibs alike are familiar with the most well-known beverage in the wizarding world: butter beer! This beverage can be served hot or cold, or can be made into a delicious fudge or ice cream for those with a sweet tooth. One of the problems I've always had with this drink is that I've found it too sweet and wanted to be done after a sip or two. By making this the same way as hot buttered rum, you're able to get the richness and a bit of sweetness, while the stoutness of the rum holds its own.

Butterbeer Cocktail, Warm

1 cup apple cider

¾ oz. butterscotch syrup (recipe on page 307)

1½ oz. Navy Strength Rum (Smith and Cross)

1 tablespoon butter batter (recipe below)

Garnish: cinnamon stick, for garnish

FOR THE BUTTER BATTER:

1 stick of butter, softened

¾ cup brown sugar

1 teaspoon cinnamon

1 teaspoon freshly grated nutmeg

Take softened butter and cream together in a standing mixer with the brown sugar, cinnamon, and nutmeg. Roll into a log shape, and wrap in parchment paper to rest.

FOR THE DRINK: In a saucepan, slowly heat the apple cider with the butterscotch syrup—you want it to be warm but not boiling. Once this has heated, add the rum to your mug, top with the warmed cider, and add the butter batter on top. Garnish with more grated nutmeg and a cinnamon stick and enjoy!

Butterscotch Syrup

1 stick of unsalted butter

1½ cups brown sugar

½ cup and 2 tablespoons heavy cream, divided

2 teaspoons vanilla extract

In a saucepan, combine butter and brown sugar over medium heat, stirring constantly to avoid burning. Once these have combined, add two tablespoons of heavy cream, whisk, and bring off heat. You want to make sure to not overheat, as this will lead to creating toffee. After the mixture has cooled, add in the remaining heavy cream and vanilla extract and whisk to incorporate. Set aside.

BUTTERBEER, CHILLED

While the Three Broomsticks pub of Harry Potter lore serves warm butter beer on tap, they also provide chilled butter beer in bottles for those who prefer their beverages on the colder side. This recipe can be made without alcohol for the little ones, but I believe the holidays should be enjoyed with a little liquid luck. For the chilled version, we can "fat wash" the liquor to help infuse more savory flavor into the drink. The process is so easy even a house elf who enjoyed a few too many butterbeers could do it (you'll want to do this about twenty-four hours in advance). First, start with whichever liquor you want to use for the cocktail. We'll stick with rum for now, but bourbon and brandy would work just fine.

Fat-washed Rum

1 stick of butter

1 bottle of aged rum (El Dorado 8 year would be a great choice)

In a saucepan, melt a stick of butter over medium heat until it starts to smell nutty and turn slightly brown. Remove from heat to cool, and combine with the rum, whisking them together. Let this cool down to room temperature, and after about two hours, freeze the mixture in an airtight container for 24 hours. The next day, you'll have a separation of the liquid and solid. Strain through a sieve or cheesecloth and you have your fat-washed rum.

Fat-washed
ButterBeer, Chilled

1½ oz. fat-washed rum (recipe on page 308)

8 oz. seltzer water (something with intense bubbles like Topo chico)

¾ oz. butterscotch syrup (recipe on page 307)

Tiny pinch of salt

Whipped cream topping, optional

Garnish: shaved nutmeg

Combine ingredients except the whipped cream (optional) and nutmeg and stir to incorporate. For the trademark foamy head, you can also whip the drink with a small electric frother, typically used for at-home lattés. Garnish with whipped cream or shaved nutmeg.

One of the drinks I was most intrigued by in the Harry Potter books was pumpkin juice. It was always available for each meal in the Great Hall, and Madame Pomfrey, Hogwarts's esteemed healer in the hospital wing, would use pumpkin juice as a healing elixir to cure various ailments. During the strained holiday season, when days and time cease to exist, I think we can all benefit from a little healing potion of our own. This recipe can be served morning or night, alongside any meal. I've included both a young wizard version, as well as one that could be found alongside butter beer in the Hog's Head Inn.

Pumpkin Elixir Punch

Serves 6–8

3 cups apple cider (homemade, or store bought if you're in a pinch)

1 (28 oz.) can pumpkin puree

2 cups Laird's Apple Brandy

¼ cup lemon juice

¼ cup apricot liqueur (Rothman and Winter would be a great choice)

Garnish: cinnamon sticks

Whisk ingredients (except cinnamon stick) together in a bowl. To serve the drinks, pour over ice in a rocks glass and garnish with a cinnamon stick "magic wand."

COCKTAILS OF THE POTIONS MASTER

"Or perhaps in Slytherin,
You'll Make your real friends,
These cunning folks use any means
To achieve their ends." —The Sorting Hat

As any young witch or wizard knows, finding out which House you will be sorted into is just as exciting as finding out which wand has chosen you (Slytherin, and holly wood, with a Phoenix core, 13" and a rigid flexibility). For someone as indecisive as me, having a hat and a wand choose *me* instead of pouring over all the options was very relaxing. When my friends and I make our cocktails for our viewing marathon, I always make sure to make a drink that really showcases the Slytherin house. Two great potions masters from the books, Severus Snape and Horace Slughorn, claim the Slytherin house as well. While Slytherins are made out to be ruthless and cruel, that simply is not true. It has been said that Slytherins and Gryffindors are very similar in their standout traits and qualities: strong leadership, resourcefulness, and a bit of arrogance. Even Harry Potter himself was almost sorted into Slytherin! I always love reading the descriptions of the Slytherin Common Room—a dungeon of sorts—partly covered by the Great Lake, with green and dark wooden accents. I always pictured the room to be relatively simple, but with an undeniable sense of luxury and sophistication. The following recipe will appear elegant while still being effortless, and could appeal to even He-Who-Must-Not-Be-Named himself!

Salazar's Collins

2 oz. Fords Gin (or any other London Dry Gin)

¾ oz. freshly squeezed lime juice

¾ oz. mint simple syrup (recipe below)

1 cucumber, shaved into thin slices, and the ends diced to muddle into the cocktail

Seltzer water, to top

Start by taking a y peeler and shave thin ribbon pieces of cucumber to wrap around the glass—hence, your snake! Watch those fingers and go slow.

Pack the glass with ice. In a shaker, muddle the diced cucumber with your other ingredients, minus the seltzer. Shake with vigor and double strain over the ice. Top with a splash of seltzer and garnish with the ribbon slices of cucumber, wrapping around the inside of the glass like a snake.

Mint Syrup

(make one day ahead of your viewing party)

1 cup sugar

1 cup water

½ cup mint leaves pulled from the stems

In a saucepan, heat the sugar and water to incorporate and immediately remove from heat. Once cooled, add the mint leaves and seal the mixture in a container with a tight-fitting lid. After infusing the mint overnight, strain and bottle the syrup. Kept in the refrigerator, the syrup will last for three weeks. Add an ounce of vodka to keep the mint syrup fresh for a few months.

Speaking of potions masters, a *Harry Potter* marathon wouldn't be complete without a little magical potion of its own. Want an easy way to impress your guests, muggles, squibs, and even witches and warlocks alike? One simple ingredient can help you take a simple, delicious cocktail and transform it into something magical: butterfly pea flower. What is this magical plant? The blue, deep indigo flowers come from the butterfly pea plant, which is a vine species native to Thailand and other surrounding areas of Southeast Asia. It has been used as a way to naturally dye foods and liquids for years. The powder, derived from the dried flowers that has been described as blue matcha, is rich in antioxidants and has purported health benefits ranging from lowering blood pressure, to supporting brain health and growth. While this powder would most likely be located in the Potions Storeroom, sneaking around Professor Snape has proved to be tricky. You can find it online or in some herbal tea stores. You can also buy the dried flowers online and use those to infuse into any liquid to change any citrus drinks' color from pale green to blue and purple. Can't find the butterfly pea flowers or powder? Never fear, as a good wizard always has another trick up their sleeve. You can also use a citric acid solution to change the color of your drink.

Butterfly Margarita Potion

2 oz. butterfly pea flower-infused Blanco Tequila of your choice (Don Fulano would be an excellent choice, recipe on page 314)

¾ oz. freshly squeezed lime juice

½ oz. Pierre Ferrand Dry Curaçao (or Curaçao of your choice)

½ oz. simple syrup

Combine ingredients in a shaker tin and shake vigorously with ice until well chilled. Strain and serve up or on the rocks with an optional salt rim.

Butterfly Pea Flower Tequila

12 oz. tequila of your choice

12 dried butterfly pea flowers

Combine the dried flowers and tequila in a jar and shake it to incorporate. Leave in a cool, dark place overnight to infuse the flowers and change the color of the liquid. The next day, strain out the flowers and bottle the tequila.

When it comes time for the marathon, you want to give yourself a full two days. I highly recommend purchasing matching onesies for you and your friends, and consulting the *Harry Potter* cookbook for some meal ideas to make it feel like you're eating in the Great Hall. Grab yourself one of Hagrid's rock cakes, a fresh mug of butterbeer, and lose yourself in the magic. Mischief Managed.

CHRISTMAS LIBATIONS FROM AROUND THE WORLD

Moose Milk

This Canadian nog variation was served to the country's military during holiday parties. No wonder they don't go to war unless we drag them into it!

2 cups cold-brew coffee

2 cups whole milk

4 cups vanilla ice cream

2 oz. bourbon

2 oz. aged rum

2 oz. vodka

Garnish: freshly grated nutmeg and shaved dark chocolate

Combine the coffee, whole milk, and ice cream in a bowl, and whisk to incorporate. You may want to let the ice cream sit out on the counter for a little while to make it easier to work with. After the coffee and dairy are combined, slowly add the booze, whisking to incorporate. To serve, pour into 6-ounce servings and add the garnish. You're ready for battle!

COLA DE MONO (CHILEAN)

The common Chilean Christmas cocktail is the Cola de Mono. Coffee-based and steeped with anise, the cocktail is typically served chilled with cream and pisco.

A more accepted chronicle of the Cola de Mono involves Chilean president Pedro Montt, monikered *el mono,* "the monkey." Legend states that President Montt asked for his sidearm with the intention of leaving a dinner party, but his host persuaded him to remain as he prepared a coffee-based concoction that restored the party's vigor.

Cola de Mono is typically served chilled during the holiday season, as it is the middle of summer at this time of the year in Chile, and temperatures can swell with little chance for snow.

Cola de Mono

2 cups cold brew

1 oz. Green Chartreuse or other herbal liqueur

1 oz. heavy cream

2 tablespoons brown sugar

4 sticks smashed and pan-toasted cinnamon

2 star anise pods

1 teaspoon shaved nutmeg

3 whole cloves

4 oz. Pisco

Heat the coffee, cream, sugar, and spice; stir, covered, at low temp for 1 hour; strain. Add Pisco to flavor. Pour over ice at room temperature, or bottle at room temperature and refrigerate.

JAMAICAN SORREL

For some folks who reside in tropical climates, cozying up to a fire with an afghan draped over your legs as steam lifts from a mug of Chartreuse Hot Chocolate (see page 323) is just a fantasy. While many of us begin dreaming about sandy beaches, palm trees, and drinks with umbrella garnishes the moment the first freeze starts to sink in, plenty of people in warmer climates yearn for a snow day, a sled, and a whiskey to sip on. The lesson of the grass being greener or the pastures more plentiful somewhere else is really just that: take me somewhere else, now! For me, Jamaica is one of those places. I've loved the music, culture, food, and drink for so long that it really feels like I've been there. If you watch the 1978 film *Rockers*, featuring many of the ineffable reggae legends from that time (highly recommended), you will also feel like you have been to Jamaica. But alas, I can only dream of the day when I'll be slaking my thirst with a hefty pour of Jamaica's own Wray and Nephew Overproof rum—a 120-proof powerhouse of white gold lightning in a bottle—and tempering it with the fuchsia-colored tart tipple known as sorrel.

I first learned about sorrel when a friend of mine, Tom Maddox, who owns Carter Creek Microgreens and supplies chefs and bartenders with all kinds of exotic herbs and flowers, told me he had a sack of hibiscus for me from a plant that just had to be cut back. He wasn't even going to charge me for it; he just wanted someone to use it. I was running a tropical rum bar at the time and began racking my brain for what I could do with a ton of hibiscus. It didn't take too many internet searches until I landed on this drink, which seemed festive, refreshing, vibrant, and, with enough Wray and Nephew rum, low-key strong.

Sorrel is the perfect holiday drink in Jamaica, due to the hibiscus flowering right around the time when it's appropriate to break out the Christmas lights. Jamaicans often make this as a punch to celebrate the Christmas holiday. Dried hibiscus flowers are also very easy to obtain and are plentiful at many Latin grocery stores. They lend a refreshing tart sensibility and the aforementioned gorgeous, vibrant red hue to any drink. This would be a great option if you're looking for something light, tart, and refreshing to celebrate the holidays. If you happen to be rum-averse, try a version of this drink with tequila. Just don't tell any of your Jamaican friends about it, okay?

Jamaican Sorrel

10 cups water

8 whole cloves

2 cinnamon sticks

1 teaspoon freshly grated nutmeg

8 oz. sorrel (dried hibiscus flowers)

½ cup ginger cordial (see page 319), or 1 cup sugar

4 oz. white rum (Wray and Nephew overproof)

3 oz. orange juice

½ oz. lime juice

2 oranges, sliced and studded with cloves

2 limes, sliced and studded with cloves

2 dashes aromatic bitters

Bring the water to a boil and add the cloves, cinnamon sticks, and nutmeg. Simmer on medium-high for 15 minutes. Promptly remove from heat. Add the sorrel and the ginger cordial or the sugar, if you're opting for a simpler version. Stir to incorporate all your ingredients, then cover and let the mixture infuse for 2 hours. After 2 hours, strain out the sorrel and spices, and add the rum, citrus, and aromatic bitters, and stir to combine. Taste for desired sweetness, adding more sugar or ginger syrup as needed. To serve, add ice to a punch bowl or pitcher and garnish with the clove-studded citrus wheels.

Ginger Cordial

2 oz. ginger, peeled and cut into small dice

2 cups sugar

1 cup water

½ cup dry white wine

½ cup Blenheim Hot Ginger Ale

½ dry cayenne pepper, roughly chopped

⅛ teaspoon kosher salt

2 tablespoons grated lemon zest (use a Microplane)

Run 1 ounce of the ginger through a juicer. You need ½ tablespoon.

Combine the ginger juice, sugar, water, white wine, and ginger ale in a medium saucepan and bring to a simmer over medium heat, stirring, about 7 minutes. Add the remaining diced ginger, cayenne pepper, and salt, reduce the heat to low, and simmer for 20 minutes to develop the flavor.

Transfer to a container, cool to room temperature, cover, and refrigerate for 3 days to infuse the cordial. Remove the cordial from the refrigerator, add the lemon zest, and stir gently for 1 minute. Strain the mixture through a fine-mesh sieve into a clean container, and discard the solids. Place a lid on the container and refrigerate. Tightly covered, the cordial will keep for up to 1 month in the refrigerator.

Though Bajans also enjoy their own version of the Jamaican sorrel drink, they also love a good egg nog riff, blended and served chilled during Christmastime. Consider this a holiday cocktail, an easy way to throw together an alternate egg nog, and a simple way to be on island time, if you can't get away to a tropical locale.

Barbados Punch-a-Cream Cocktail

Serves 4

8 oz. Bajan rum like Plantation

4 eggs

1 can sweetened condensed milk

1 teaspoon vanilla extract

½ oz. banana liqueur (try Tempus Fugit)

½ oz. lime juice

Garnish: shaved nutmeg

Add the rum, eggs, condensed milk, vanilla, and banana liqueur in a blender and blend on low to incorporate. Add the lime juice and a cup of crushed ice and blend until smooth. Serve in festive glasses with nutmeg shaved over the top.

Bajan Hot Chocolate

1½ oz. Bajan rum

1 oz. rum cream (see page 298)

5 oz. hot chocolate

1 dash aromatic bitters (or Angostura Cocoa bitters)

Garnish: whipped cream

Add the rum and whiskey cream to a warm mug of hot chocolate, and stir to combine. Add the aromatic bitters and stir them in. Garnish with whipped cream.

HOT CHOCOLATE AND GANACHE

The easiest way to improve your homemade hot chocolate game is by making a ganache, essentially a dark chocolate topping that can be used on desserts, in coffee drinks, and to bolster winter cocktails. You don't need many ingredients to make a quality ganache. What you don't want to skimp on is good chocolate. In Nashville, we're lucky to have an amazing chocolate maker, Olive and Sinclair, and all of their stone-ground baking chocolates are amazing for making a ganache. One hack we can offer is to use a spirit that either reminds you of chocolate, goes well with chocolate, or flat-out has chocolate tasting notes. I love green chartreuse with chocolate so I'm going to use that and a new release from Woodford Reserve, "Chocolate Malt" whiskey.

Chartreuse Ganache

1 cup heavy cream

10 oz. good dark chocolate, chopped (we love the aforementioned Olive and Sinclair chocolate)

½ oz. Green Chartreuse

1 oz. Bourbon (Woodford Reserve's Chocolate Malt, if you can find it)

Heat the cream over medium heat, slowly bringing it to a boil and watching it the whole time (it can quickly boil over and become a mess in a few seconds). As it begins to boil, remove from heat and add the chocolate. Return to medium low heat and whisk in the chocolate. Add the booze and keep whisking. For hot chocolate cocktails, you can thin out the ganache with more heavy cream, half and half, or water. Allow the chocolate to cool before storing in a container with a tight-fitting lid in the refrigerator.

Chartreuse Hot Chocolate with Absinthe Whipped Cream

1½ oz. bourbon

1 ½ oz. Chartreuse ganache (see page 322)

6 oz. hot milk or water (less for a richer hot chocolate)

1 dash Angostura or cinnamon bitters (page 116)

Shaken whipped cream with a ½ oz. of absinthe added

Tiny pinch of salt

Add the bourbon and ganache to a hot mug filled with the water or milk. Dash in the bitters and stir briskly to combine the ingredients. Add a tiny pinch of salt and top with the absinthe whipped cream.

For the absinthe cream: in a cocktail shaker combine 4 ounces of heavy cream with the absinthe and shake until properly whipped.

Coffee Bitters (to go with all that Chocolate)

1 32-oz. Mason jar

6 oz. cinnamon sticks, crushed and toasted (using a digital scale)

2 star anise pods

4 cloves

2 allspice berries (whole)

30 oz. 100-proof vodka

2 cups coarse-ground coffee

1 tablespoon gentian root (available from Mountain Rose Herbs and other online retailers)

Zest of one orange, dried (zest an orange and dry on a plate on your countertop overnight)

4 oz. rich demerara syrup (see page 196)

Using the back of a cast-iron skillet on a firm countertop, crush the cinnamon sticks. Then add the rest of the dry spices and crush together with the cinnamon. Add the spices to a skillet over medium-low heat and toast lightly, taking care not to overcook or burn the spices. Transfer them to a plate to allow them to cool.

Once cooled, add them to a 32-ounce Mason jar, along with the coffee, gentian, vodka, and dried orange zest, and let sit in a cool, dry place in your kitchen away from sunlight. As often as once a day (or a little less if the day gets away from you), shake the mixture briskly to get as much extraction from your botanicals as possible. Taste the mixture every 3 or 4 days to see how the flavor increases. After 3 weeks, if you're happy with the extraction and intensity of the flavor, strain out the solids through cheesecloth and add the rich demerara syrup. The bitters will keep for at least a year.

Booze News CHOCOLATE

CHOCOLATE DAY

National Chocolate Day is October 28; International Chocolate Day is celebrated on September 13, commemorating the birth date of Milton Hershey.

CHOCOLATE FARTS

A French inventor, Christian Poincheval, has invented a pill that makes farts smell like chocolate. With a history in homeopathy, Poincheval's supplement utilizes all-natural ingredients including fennel, cacao, seaweed, bilberry, and plant resin. Inspired by a gassy dinner with friends, Poincheval set out to improve the negative stigma associated with farting, keeping the gas and minimizing the ass. Partnering with friend Lutin Malin, the chocolate fart pills are now available online, along with a slew of other "flavors," including ginger, violet, lily of the valley, and rose.

SANTA ALWAYS WINS

According to the *Guinness Book of World Records*, the largest gathering of Santa's elves was at the Siam Paragon Mall in Bangkok, Thailand, on November 25, 2014. The participants ranged in age from 9 to 15 years, and the gathering netted 1,762 little pixies. Another 14 were disqualified for inaccurate wardrobe. Contrastingly, the largest gathering of Santa Clauses occurred on December 27 of the same year in Tritur, India. It eclipsed the elven population with a total draw of 18,112.

CHRISTMAS IN WEST AFRICA

In the Republic of Senegal, in West Africa, with a 95 percent Muslim population, Christmas is very much celebrated. In the capital, Dakar, street vendors add tassels, garlands, and Christmas trees to their repertoire. Businesses decorate accordingly; in fact, Santa Clauses are as prevalent as mosques.

This all stems from Senegal's secular stance on government and religion. An overwhelming harmony of religious diversity has long been one of the country's greatest strengths. In fact, it is not uncommon for members of a family to practice different religions.

Celebrating each other's diversity will always be the keystone of unity.

No celebration in Senegal is complete without the consumption of bissap, a spiced tea made from the flowers of the sorrel shrub. Rich in oxalic acid, sorrel provides a slightly bitter sour flavor, tickling your saliva glands into overproduction. Cooked down with cinnamon, clove, ginger, and citrus, it is perfect for a hot summer morning on the rocks in a coffee cup on the porch, or heated and consumed fireside in the autumn/winter. Most Senegalese do not imbibe in alcohol; however, on my porch there's no better pairing than a slightly aged Caribbean rum.

Bissap

2 cups bissap (sorrel or roselle or hibiscus flowers)

3 liters (about 3.2 quarts) water

½ cup sugar

1 tablespoon grated ginger

Clean the sorrel leaves by rinsing them under cold water. Bring one liter of water to a boil, and cook leaves for 20 minutes, then strain into a large bowl. Add the strained bits of sorrel or roselle or hibiscus back to the pot, and add another liter of water and bring to a simmer. Lightly simmer for 15 minutes, strain the mixture into the bowl, and add the strained bits back to the pot again and add the other liter of water. Let sit without cooking for 20 minutes, and strain that mixture into the large bowl. Add sugar and ginger to taste and your favorite spirit!

CHRISTMAS COCKTAILS

The Tree Hugger

The Christmas Tree Cocktail

- 1½ oz. botanical gin, preferably St. George Terroir
- 1 tablespoon Virginia Pine Syrup (recipe follows)
- ¼ oz. fresh lemon juice
- ¼ oz. fresh lime juice
- ½ oz. Green Chartreuse (or make your own, page 332)
- 1 dash Lovage Bitters (see page 181)
- 1 oz. Rosemary Tincture (recipe follows), in a small spray bottle, for spritzing the drink
- Garnish: 1 rosemary sprig

Combine the gin, pine syrup, lemon juice, lime juice, chartreuse, and bitters in a shaker, fill halfway with ice, and shake vigorously until well chilled. Strain into a rocks glass with 2 large ice cubes, spray once with the tincture, garnish with the rosemary sprig, and serve.

Virginia Pine Syrup

- 1 cup sugar
- 1 cup water
- ½ cup 1-inch-long pieces Virginia pine needles, washed and dried
- 1½ tablespoons grated lemon zest (use a Microplane)

Combine the sugar and water in a small saucepan, and bring the

mixture to a simmer over medium heat, stirring to dissolve the sugar, about 5 minutes. Remove from the stove and cool to room temperature. Transfer to a clean quart canning jar and add the pine needles and lemon zest. Wipe the rim and threads clean, place the lid and ring on, tighten the ring, and let the syrup infuse for 4 days in the refrigerator.

Strain the syrup through a fine-mesh sieve into a clean quart canning jar and discard the solids. Wipe the rim and threads clean, place the lid and ring on, tighten the ring, and refrigerate. Tightly covered, the syrup will keep for up to 3 weeks in the refrigerator.

Rosemary Tincture

2 cups fresh rosemary leaves

1 teaspoon dried rosemary

1 cup 100-proof vodka

Combine all the ingredients in a clean pint canning jar, wipe the rim and threads clean, place the lid and ring on, tighten the ring, and store the tincture in a cool, dark area with a maximum temperature of 75°F for 2 weeks, shaking the mixture every other day to infuse the tincture.

Strain the tincture through a fine-mesh sieve lined with cheesecloth into a clean pint canning jar and discard the solids. Wipe the rim and threads clean, place the lid and ring on, tighten the ring, and store the tincture at room temperature. Tightly covered, the tincture will keep for up to 4 months in a dark place at room temperature.

Liquid Gold Chartreuse

¼ cup dried lemon verbena

¼ cup dried lemon balm

¼ cup dried chamomile

2 tablespoons grated lemon zest (use a Microplane)

1 tablespoon grated lime zest (use a Microplane)

1 tablespoon angelica root

1 teaspoon dandelion root

1 teaspoon pink peppercorns

1 teaspoon saffron

¼ teaspoon dill weed

2 cardamom pods, cracked

1 star anise pod

120 oz. 100-proof vodka

¼ cup local honey

Combine all the ingredients, except for the vodka and honey, in a clean 1-gallon glass jar. Add the vodka and cover with the lid. Swirl the jar to incorporate all the ingredients. Store the mixture undisturbed in a cool, dark area for 2 weeks.

Strain the chartreuse through a fine-mesh sieve lined with cheesecloth into a clean 1-gallon glass jar, add the honey, and stir to combine completely. Transfer the chartreuse to 4 clean quart canning jars, wipe the rims and threads clean, place the lids and rings on, tighten the rings, and store the chartreuse at room temperature. Tightly covered, the chartreuse will keep for up to a year in a dark place at room temperature.

Christmas Cobbler

2 teaspoons castor sugar (superfine sugar)

One 1-inch x 2-inch piece lemon peel, pith removed

One 1-inch x 2-inch piece orange peel, pith removed

2 dashes aromatic bitters

1½ oz. amontillado sherry

1½ oz. Madeira

2 cups crushed ice

Garnish: basil and mint leaves

One ¼-inch-thick slice of orange

1 lemon twist

3 blackberries, raspberries, or blueberries Combine the sugar, lemon peel, orange peel, and bitters in a shaker, and muddle gently. Add the sherry and Madeira and stir to combine. Fill the shaker with ice, and shake vigorously until well chilled.

Fill a julep cup with the crushed ice, and strain the cocktail into the cup. Garnish the drink with the orange slice, lemon twist, berries, and basil and mint, if using, and serve with a straw.

CHRISTMAS
COBBLER
p. 333

SNOW COCKTAILS AND THE SNOW-GRONI

One of the most enjoyable things about a snow day is when you suddenly find yourself off work, with nothing to do but shovel the steps and build a fire in the fireplace. When you finish whatever menial tasks you set out for yourself on this cozy day—getting the kids bundled up, making more coffee—you may be scratching your head wondering, "Should I start drinking?" We don't judge; all we want to remind you is happy hour never starts before lunch. That's our only rule when it comes to day drinking.

One thing to remember about making cocktails at home is the need for ice, which chills your cocktails to the bone and provides proper dilution, opening up the flavor of what's in your glass. This is bare bones cocktail wisdom: you can never forget the water component of your drink. Most cocktails contain about one ounce of water. But what if you're getting that ice/water combination from fresh snow? Making snow cocktails (even zero proof drinks for the kiddos) can be a fun way to pass the time, as snow can chill your cocktail very quickly and provide a light, fluffy texture to everything from a margarita to an old-fashioned or negroni (recipe on next page). For the snow-to-water ratio, we'll look to a conversion chart created by NASA. That's right, your day drinking activity just became a science project! According to NASA, the snow-to-water ratio depends on the temperature of the air, so you can use this table:

+ 30° F—10:1 ratio snow to water

+ 25° F—15:1 ratio snow to water

+ 18° F—20:1 ratio snow to water

+ 12° F—30:1 ratio snow to water

If it's much colder than that, maybe just stay inside and use your blender. The most important thing when making drinks is to have fun with it. Enjoy this sno-groni recipe and use it to tailor your ratios to any of your favorite cocktails.

Snow-Groni

1 oz. sweet vermouth, chilled

3 cups fresh snow, plus more to top

1 oz. Campari or other red bitter

1 oz. gin

Light pinch of salt

Garnish: orange twist, slices, and a cherry

In a rocks glass or Collins glass, add the snow and cold sweet vermouth (pulled from the refrigerator), before adding the gin and Campari. Sprinkle a little salt on top and add more snow. Garnish with an orange peel or twist and a cherry. This drink is most enjoyable with a straw.

TWELVE

A Christmas Short Story— "Rickshaw Road"

Cynthia strode across the crowded dining room like the ballet dancer she wished she still was. To watch her in complete command over her section at the small but busy bistro I bussed tables at during my semester abroad in Paris, was a thing of beauty.

There was a lot to see looking out my perch between the espresso machine and the duck press we never used, as the windows opened out onto busy streets filled with young couples holding hands, old men carrying newspapers, and stylish women with long overcoats. Christmas lights were being strung out on the street around the tops of lampposts as if the sky was multiplying in stars. Through the far right window I could see a corner of the River Seine, just beyond the boulevard where below the street, vendors would sell books, clothes, and other knick-knacks that I'd peruse when I wasn't working, studying, or out drinking. But mostly my gaze was fixed on Cynthia. She was named after a peninsula in Northeastern Ontario, Canada, where her mother grew up, and tolerated my broken high school French while supremely enjoying talking trash to me in English. Her black hair had flecks of blue and her tall, slender, statuesque frame had the quiet confidence of an athlete.

"Women don't like poetry," Cynthia said as she flew by me on her way back to the kitchen with a clutch of dishes. I dashed to the table she was clearing and grabbed as many plates as I could, neatly stacking the silverware on the top plate *away* from the guests before I dashed back into the kitchen. "Men think we do, but it's a myth, actually," she continued once I was fully in earshot.

"Ok, alright . . . I'm sure there are plenty of women," I stammered before she cut me off.

"Yes, yes, you're right, there are," she quickly added with her index finger waving in front of my face, which was slowly turning red. "It's just that none of them like poetry, ok? There are other ways to a woman's heart."

I had made the unfortunate decision, under the influence of gin—you could say I was "ginfluenced" a lot that semester in Paris—to show Cynthia some poetry I had written for her. While it was no surprise to her how I felt, the poetry did something unexpected from my vantage point.

> If I could go to this peninsula in Ontario
> where you got your name
> I'd look into every woman's eyes

and ask them to dance with me until dawn
but I'd only be thinking of you
seeing your face in every stone
but that's nothing new

It made her mad. "You think you can swoop in from fucking America and seduce some French girl who's older, smarter, and can probably kick your ass?" was her quick and succinct review of said poetry. She later softened. "You're sweet, but I can't tell if you're the dumbest or the smartest one in the room sometimes." It was not the response I was hoping for.

I had never met a knockout librarian before
all graceful sweaters, intense chess-game eyes
and intelligence you wore on your brow
like a badge of honor earned from the hard-won
wisdom of past lives well-lived.
I was always jealous of librarians,
perched as they were in their quiet domains of discourse.
The all-knowing gaze that I longed to
be lost in, to ask "know me better than I know myself,
but leave out the bad parts," and point me to the book
that will finally inspire me
to write you into existence.
Because you can't be real

Didn't like that one, either. "I *am* real, twat," she whispered to me one night during service. And she was, so real. "And what's with the obsession with librarians? I can introduce you to one, you know."

Back in the kitchen, she was still coaching me through my pursuit... of her. I hadn't written much poetry for anyone at that point.

"Premier temp," I said, unwisely trying out some French since the cooks couldn't hear me.

"Ohhhhh no no no," she quickly swooped in, and the finger was back wagging in my face again. "So, you say in America, 'stay in your lane?' Are you trying to say it was your first time? Your first time writing poetry? You would say 'premier fois,' you silly ass. Is this your first time trying to get laid, too? I feel for you, ma douce."

"Can we still go to Monk's after work?" I said, changing the subject. "Maybe there's a girl there who doesn't mind terrible French."

"Of course! What else are we going to do? Besides, we're going to miss you on Christmas," she said with suddenly warm eyes as she pushed her hands into the wall behind her to springboard herself back into the dining room. Feeling homesick and with no plans to travel back home to New York for the Christmas holiday, I was apprehensive for my first Christmas away from my parents. I'd be meeting my two brothers—both studying abroad as well—Frank in Florence, Italy, and Adam in Barcelona, for a three-day excursion to Dublin, Ireland, where we'd mix it up in the pubs, drink copious pints of Guinness, and make a few new Christmas memories. Or at least that's what we had in mind . . .

* * * * * * * * *

Frank clutched his duffel bag tightly with his right hand as he and his tattered Mets hat rose from the tiny taxi that brought him from the train station to the hostel where we were shacking up, near the famous Temple Bar in Dublin. He was twenty years old and stood 6'1" and, in his few months in Italy, had developed a taste for pretty much anything his Italian house mom would make. His taut, lean frame now resembled the puffy indifference of an actor gaining weight for a role.

"That wasn't bad, I should have fucking walked and saved some cash," Frank said as he bounded up to my brother Adam and I, standing outside the Kinlay Hostel. He gave us a double hug as he looked up at the hostel's sign and remarked, "Kinlay. I guess this is where the kin lay their heads huh?"

"Good one," said Adam, meaning it. "Merry Christmas idiot, I see you can't let go of that Mets hat." My brother Adam, the oldest and wisest of the bunch at twenty-three, a tall, handsome drink of water with a thick head of rusty brown hair certainly not inherited from our father, was the voice of reason and the one we looked to in times of uncertainty. Having dropped out of college for a brief period to work on an oyster boat in the Gulf, Adam had a wide gaze and a sensibility beyond his age. He was in his final year of college and his fall in Barcelona was shrouded in mystery, which meant he had met a woman and it was getting serious. At twenty-one years old and running out of money before Christmas, I was the middle child with all of the insecurities that came with it.

"Look at you, Chrissy, you look good man. How's Paris treating you, you romantic little fuck? Still working at the restaurant?" Frank said to me as I noticed his weary, bloodshot eyes from all the holiday traveling.

"He's Christopher now," said Adam, smiling. "And he only works there because of this girl, Cynthia. He wrote some poetry for her, didn't go well," he added, rubbing his eyes in brotherly shame. "Now you're caught up Frankie, let's go get some beers." It was ten past noon.

After Frank dropped his bag off and threw some water on his face, it was time to hit the town with the hunger, thirst, and lust of three Americans freed from the nostalgic trappings of Christmas with the family in Yonkers. Our goal was to begin and end our night at the Temple Bar, a grand pub dating back to 1840, painted in gorgeous red trim, outlined in greenery with hanging plants above the façade and, during this time of year, adorned from head to toe in glowing Christmas lights with a giant, tall red Christmas tree hovering at the nexus of the corner pub. It was a sight to behold, even in the light of day. Adam tipped us off to the Temple Bar—he the ever-curious traveler who always did his research—noting there was a large bronze statue of James Joyce inside the bar. "I know you've always wanted to have a whiskey with James Joyce," read his text a few weeks earlier. "Here's your chance." As we walked slowly through the hallowed halls of the Temple Bar, looking the part of American tourists with tousled hair, careful not to disturb the warm, low-hanging lamps, we settled on a table near the Joyce statue, where some British tourists were taking pictures and hamming it up.

"He'd hate that, huh Chrissy?" said Adam under his breath, but also to me.

We ordered the famous "Toastie" sandwich, a perfectly constructed masterpiece of hot ham and cheese, with vine tomatoes and spring onions on sourdough bread. "This is insane," read Frank's hushed, reverent review. It wasn't the last Toastie we'd have on that trip. We washed it all down with two quick beers each and a shot of the house whiskey (Temple bottled their own blends of 10-, 12-, and 15-year Irish whiskey), which Adam noted was aged in bourbon barrels from America. "We can't escape ourselves, can we?" he said in his philosophical gaze. "Powers is the cheap Irish whiskey, that's what we'll be drinking later tonight." And with that we slid out of our chairs, as our buzzed bodies bent towards the sun lowering over the city, through the old window shades that showed the city as if just beyond a dressing room door. In the afternoon's overcast silvery glow, we set out to find a pool table and take in whatever Dublin had in store.

The rest of the day and evening became quite a blur to us all, though we're certain we spent much of the evening on a rooftop bar adjacent to Temple, talking and drinking with some oddly tanned (this was Ireland, after all) American students from the University of Alabama. By the time we ended up back at the Temple Bar, I suppose we began to look over the whiskey list, led by Adam's sudden curiosity about really expensive Irish whiskey. It was the night before the night before Christmas, and it felt like every single patron in the Temple Bar wanted to get really drunk, sing '90s music, and watch old rugby games. After Frank slipped us all some weed gummies from his train trip to Amsterdam, things only became *slower*. It was before 1 a.m., we'd all had at least three "Toasties" sandwiches on the day as we all gave each other the look that said, "let's get the fuck out of here before somebody gets hurt, throws up, or falls on their face." We plunged into the fresh air and drunkenly dug through our pockets for the European cigarettes we'd all taken to as smokers on holiday. Before Frank could get his lit, he swayed and gave me another look, "It's comin' up, I'm in trouble." Adam noticed, nodded, and yelled, "Just do it dude! You'll be better off . . . here," as he brought him to the curbside street drain and Frank let it fly. I was laughing and enjoying the Christmas light haze until the last thing I remember, which was a look of scorn from a woman who seemed disgusted by my swaying disposition, a local who looked into my soul and did not like what she saw.

The next morning my eyelids pounded my temples like tiny fists of fury drumming into my skull as I noticed the harsh light of 10:30 a.m. outside our hostel's front window. We had missed free breakfast—strange sausage of some kind—and I had the sinking feeling in my stomach like something had gone wrong, but I'd never really find out what it was. Frank was up, looking at his phone, with a freshly showered glow and an enviable "yeah, I'm the guy who threw up," taut look on his face. Adam had Frank's hat over his face and was sleeping, or pretending to. I grabbed my pants and rifled through the pockets to see how much money I had for breakfast, and swallowed a lump in my throat when I couldn't find a single piece of cash in my wallet or pockets.

"Did I get . . . the drinks last night?" I asked, hesitating a little.

"You were buying rounds of 8 Guinness . . . Guinness's . . . Wait, so if it's plural Guinness is it 'Guinneye'? 'Guineii'? I'm not sure how you would spell it, I'll leave that to you Chrissy. But yeah, you bought a ton of beers at the rooftop," said Frank, somewhat lucidly recalling the details.

"Well, we have to get some breakfast; it's Christmas Eve. We've got the dinner to go to but shit . . . I don't think I can use my card tonight. Adam!" I said, louder to see if he'd rouse awake. The hat shuffled on his head and he emerged ever so slightly, with a few new wrinkles on his cheek from sleeping on his jacket. He yawned immediately and slowly lowered to the floor.

"What . . . man," said Adam, letting out a big breath and slowly falling asleep again.

"How much cash do you have on you? We need to get some breakfast and begin the healing process," I said louder, like talking to an older relative who left their hearing aid in the other room.

"Relax man, I got you. Shut up though," he said before grinning and closing his eyes again.

"Frank, can we get some breakfast?" I arose in last night's clothes and grabbed the empty trash can sitting on the floor, flung open the door and stumbled into our door out into the hallway of the hostel. Walking down the narrow, slanted hallway that looked like something out of an experimental French film from the '70s, I searched for the ice machine I was sure I had seen at some point the previous night. After filling up the little waste basket, I retreated back to the room and dumped the ice into the sink and began filling it with water. Once full, I dunked my head into the ice and immediately felt my head regain some consciousness as I realized yet again that I was broke, and my brothers weren't much better off. I had three nights of tips waiting for me at the restaurant, a paycheck a few days away, and a debit card with overdraft fees clinging to the balance.

"We're not calling mom and dad, assholes," said Adam, rising from the dead. "We'll get a rickshaw and fuckin ferry people around for a while tonight. We'll make a killing because we're the weird American dudes running a rickshaw on Christmas Eve in fucking Dublin. What is wrong with this plan?"

"Sorry if I hadn't considered a rickshaw, brother," said Frank bewildered, "But what the fuck are you even talking about?"

"My buddy Leonard had to do it for a few nights when he got caught up in some late-night blackjack game near the Riverwalk back in 2016," said Adam, always armed with a story none of us could verify. "You pay like thirty euro, and if you make forty euro or more, you pay them the thirty euro. If you make less than thirty euro you don't have to pay 'em shit, you just give the rickshaw back."

"What are we, in 1934?" queried Frank. "We're talkin' rickshaws and if you don't make a certain amount you just bring it back and don't pay the rental fee? This is some weird shit."

"You're saying a tourist can just rent a rickshaw, charge people money for it, take cash from people, and then go spend it at the bars? Why isn't everyone doing this right now?" I asked as the voice of reason.

"Fuck 'em if they're not, man," said Adam, awake and armed with a plan all in about five minutes. "We're going to. And we're gonna make Christmas memories for the people of Dublin tonight fellas." His eyes glowed with a haze, as he cracked a smile. "We're gonna make a killing, and probably meet some women too. You're welcome."

"Don't get ahead of yourself, let's get some food first. Fuckin rickshaw," said Frank, grabbing his hat back.

* * * * * * * * *

Frank and I didn't even want to know where one could get a rickshaw on Christmas Eve in Dublin, while Adam seemed keen on venturing out on his own to acquire said rickshaw during the afternoon. He asked us to meet him in front of a riverside bar called the Workman's Room at five o'clock sharp. His last words to us were "I'll take it as far as I can but trust me, this is a three-man operation so don't fuck around and be late grabbing beers or something." He skipped backwards a little, turned, and was off. Frank and I looked at each other wondering, "was he planning this?"

At 5 p.m. sharp, Frank and I arrived on the steps outside the Workman's Room, laughing our asses off as my brother slowly pulled the large, wooden rickshaw up next to the curb, with thick wooden beams and worn, monster-truck size tires that looked like they wouldn't last through the night.

"That thing won't make it through the night. There's no way, brother," said Frank as he busted up.

Adam's eyes bulged with the reality of the situation. "You want to stay in the hostel all night on Christmas Eve or do you wanna have some fun?" It wasn't a question, really. We chose the latter.

We devised our strategy that night based on the many three-on-three basketball games we had played back in Yonkers. I would run the point, which was essentially riding in the rickshaw and attracting customers, navigating from my phone, and running beside to tell our customers our family story and whatever bullshit we could come up with about Dublin, while my oxen brothers would pull the rickshaw, toggling back between "lead puller" and "steady backer," as we called them. During our first few practice runs down the alley, we realized that we could move pretty fast if we needed to, just not for very long.

Our first customers were easy enough, a couple from Belfast who needed to cross the river to yet another row of bars, before heading to a Christmas party back on the other side. I told them to text me when they wanted to be picked back up and we'd do our best to accommodate. Early in the evening, the tips were generous as spirits remained on a holiday high among the clientele. Christmas lights sparkled all over the city as warm, rosy faces spilled out from the pubs into the streets where bodies began to sway a little more with each passing hour. In the beautiful old Dublin cathedrals Christmas carols and hymns rang out and we looked at each other in that way that only siblings can—we were lucky to be together, making a new memory in a place we'd never been, doing something we'd never done. With a little money under our belts, we decided to break for dinner. We had discounted tickets to a show near our hostel, which included a sandwich if you bought a beer, but they were just a throw-in for staying at the hostel and we didn't think much of it. Now that we had money to burn, discounts were of no use to us. We bellied up to the closest pub we could find, a place called the Bad Ass Café, which apparently had comedy shows and smartass bartenders, but notably sported one of those curved arm rests ringing the bar, the lip where you can rest your arms while your beer stays on a coaster at a comfortable distance. We ordered pints of Guinness, shots of whiskey, and pastrami sandwiches. After that we tried the mussels with garlic bread, followed by two dozen briny oysters, generously brightened with a big squeeze of lemon from Adam's hand. We paid the tab with a good portion of our rickshaw money and stole back out into the night for the second shift.

"Oh shit! No way . . . dude, the fuckin rickshaw is gone!" said Frank looking back at Adam who had a look like he already knew and was glancing around the street in all directions.

"Frankie, you head that way," said Adam pointing left. "Chris, you take the alleyway; I'll head this way. Walk for like ten minutes then head back to this spot if you don't see it anywhere. Yell out 'rickshaw!' if you find it or see who's riding it."

Just as I started down the alley, I could make out the rickshaw about eighty yards ahead, but it seemed to be coming back towards us.

"Yo! I see it!" I yelled out to Adam and Frank who were still in earshot. "It's headed back this way!"

"What is it, driving itself!?" shouted Adam as he ran over. Frank ran over and took off his hat, scratching his head as he squinted through the street lights.

"Dad!? No fuckin way," said Frank, shooting us a look as we squinted through the shadows and tried to make sense of the situation. "Guys, it's Dad! What are you doing here!?"

Emerging from the shadows, pulling the rickshaw and smiling like a crocodile, our dad, a burly six foot two with a salt and pepper Santa Claus beard, sporting his old newsboy cap, a thick cream-colored sailor sweater, and a long navy overcoat, strode up into the neon beerlight filling the street corner to our stunned momentary silence.

"I couldn't let my sons do Dublin on Christmas Eve without their Dad, who gave 'em their Irish in the first place! Merry Christmas, my boys."

"Holy shit, where's Mom?" was all I could get out as I grabbed my dad's hand to shake it and he pulled me in for a hug.

"She's at the hotel resting. She wants us all to come back there and drink some Champagne in the bar. Think you can handle that Frankie? Adam knew about all of this, by the way," he said motioning around to nothing in particular like he always did. "We got delayed by about six hours; we were hoping to do dinner but had to eat some kind of TV dinner on the plane. I got a message from Adam to come to this area and look for a rickshaw he rented. Can somebody please tell me: what's the deal with this rickshaw?"

Everyone laughed, beaming as we all shook our heads in disbelief. "Adam had an idea to make some money carting this thing around," said Frank.

"Well . . . You've got your last customer of the night. Let's get to the hotel and have some bubbly. It's Christmas Eve," said Dad. And with that he stepped up onto the rickshaw looking like a fashionable Santa who also ran a shrimp boat.

"Ok, if you say so. Here we go!" Adam and Frank took their positions as I charted a course for the hotel.

"Take me to the Westbury Hotel, my good men! I'm thirsty," said our last customer of the night.

"Oh damn, the Westbury?" said Adam, turning around. "Fancy."

"Turn this thing around, we're headed away from the river," I said staring at my phone.

We set out into the cold, twinkling Dublin streets, passing couples arm in arm, drunk friends holding each other up, and locals in Santa hats walking briskly. As we picked up speed, I trotted next to the rickshaw and looked over at my dad, who was smiling at me. Moments later we passed a fight spilling out from a corner pub as three men were shoving each other and alliances were hard to make out.

"This town never changes," said Dad.

We pulled up to the rounded street entrance at the Westbury as Christmas lights glowed from the inside and out of the grand hotel. We helped my dad down from the rickshaw and he gave the bellhop some cash saying, "Keep an eye on the cart, my good man."

"It's a rickshaw, Dad," said Frank, chuckling.

Inside, a piano twinkled "Silent Night" as we strolled through the lobby looking for the bar. As I scanned the room, I noticed a hand out-stretched from a long couch, as if cheersing the air, holding a flute of champagne. It was Mom.

"Hiyeeeeeee!" squealed mom in her unmistakable joy, rising from the large lobby sofa. "My boys are here!"

We dashed over as Frank picked up Mom and spun her around, nearly knocking over the bottle of bubbly sitting in a gold bucket of ice that was perched in a stand next to the sofa.

"We need four glasses," said my dad, holding up four fingers to the nearest person with a uniform on. My mom hugged all of us individually and pulled back each time, noting what had changed about us in the four short months abroad. "Frank is eating well, I see," she said to me. "Is Chrissy doing ok?" I heard her ask Adam. We sat down in the plush chairs adjacent to the sofa and all took a breath. Glasses arrived and Dad, who insisted on pouring, grabbed the bottle from its bath of ice and began pouring quickly as bubbles spilled out from the glasses and onto the floor.

"To family and being together," my dad said as he raised his glass higher than any of us could reach.

We clinked glasses and took a sip before sitting down in the warm glow of the lobby Christmas tree. Through my glass, the bubbles rose continuously while snow began to fall outside the large windows adorned with huge wreaths decked out in red lights. "What do you want for Christmas, Mom?" said Frank.

"This," she said.

New
Year,
New
Brews

THIRTEEN

New Year's Eve— Beyond the French 75

(BUT THAT, TOO)

You can't really discuss New Year's and Champagne cocktails without discussing one of the most popular and crowd-pleasing sparkling wine drinks, the French 75.

Now considered a light, dainty drink fit for bachelorettes and cool moms, the French 75 is actually a flavor-bomb powerhouse when made as intended. This drink is named after the French army's favorite weapon used throughout World War I, the 75-millimeter light field gun, of which 20,000 were in use during the war. Over 200 million shells were fired from the gun over a five-year period in WWI, and the gun could fire off fifteen rounds of ammo per minute. As word spread of the weapon's prowess and success on the battlefield, bartenders began making drinks in tribute. The first iteration (recipe to follow) combined gin with apple brandy and plenty of sparkling wine and, according to *Difford's Guide*, was declared "the most powerful drink in the world," hitting with "remarkable precision." The drink would change over the following decades, with other versions including absinthe and curacao. It's quite the origin story for a drink now considered to be a brunch gal classic, and one that (in our humble experience) men are often too insecure to order. Let's call it progress that we don't name cocktails for artillery weapons anymore. What follows are some of our favorite French 75 riffs and a host of sparkling wine cocktails to get you going on New Year's Eve.

Original French 75 Cocktail (the Soixante-Quinze)

1½ oz. gin

1 oz. apple brandy

¾ oz. fresh lemon juice

½ oz. grenadine (see page 56)

1 dash **Angostura or cinnamon bitters**

Pinch of Maldon sea salt

Sparkling wine, to top

Garnish: lemon twist

Combine everything except the sparkling wine and garnish in a cocktail shaker and shake vigorously until well chilled. Strain into a coupe or flute glass and top with plenty of good sparkling wine. Garnish with a lemon twist.

French 75 Punch

Serves 4

6 oz. gin

2 oz. Cocchi Americano or Lillet

12 oz. lemonade

4 dashes aromatic bitters

1 bottle sparkling wine

Garnish: lemon twist

Place all ingredients, except for the sparkling wine and garnish, in a punch bowl and stir to combine. When it's time to serve, add ice and pour in the bottle of sparkling wine. Stir and garnish.

French 75 Cocktail

2 oz. gin

¾ oz. fresh lemon juice

¾ oz. simple syrup

1 dash Angostura or cinnamon bitters

Pinch of Maldon sea salt

Sparkling wine, to top

Garnish: lemon twist

Combine everything except the sparkling wine and garnish in a cocktail shaker and shake vigorously until well chilled. Strain into a coupe or flute glass and top with plenty of good sparkling wine. Garnish with a lemon twist.

Cognac French 75

2 oz. cognac or brandy

¾ oz. fresh lemon juice

½ oz. simple syrup

1 barspoon orange curacao

1 dash Angostura or cinnamon bitters

Pinch of Maldon sea salt

Sparkling wine, to top

Garnish: lemon twist

Combine everything except the sparkling wine and garnish in a cocktail shaker and shake vigorously until well chilled. Strain into a coupe or flute glass and top with plenty of good sparkling wine. Garnish with a lemon twist.

MORE OF OUR FAVORITE SPARKLING WINE COCKTAILS, GREAT FOR A NEW YEAR'S SOIREE.

The Old Cuban

6 mint leaves, 1 reserved for garnish

2 oz. gold rum

¾ oz. lime juice

¾ oz. simple syrup

1 dash Angostura or cinnamon bitters

Pinch of Maldon sea salt

Sparkling wine, to top

Garnish: mint leaf

Lightly muddle five mint leaves in a shaker tin. Combine everything except the sparkling wine and garnish in the shaker and shake vigorously until well chilled. Double-strain (to strain the bits of mint out) into a coupe or flute glass and top with plenty of good sparkling wine. Garnish with a mint leaf.

The Seelbach No. 2

1 ½ oz. rye whiskey

½ oz. Pierre Ferrand dry curacao

4 dashes Peychaud's bitters

4 dashes Angostura or cinnamon bitters

Pinch of Maldon sea salt

Sparkling wine, to top

Garnish: orange twist

Combine everything except the sparkling wine and garnish in a mixing glass filled with ice and stir until well chilled. Strain into a coupe or flute glass and top with plenty of good sparkling wine. Garnish with an orange twist.

Death in the Afternoon (A Hemingway staple)

1 oz. absinthe

Sparkling wine, to top

Garnish: lemon twist

In a mixing glass filled with ice, add the absinthe and stir briskly. As the absinthe changes color to a milky opalescence, strain the absinthe into a chilled coupe. Top with sparkling wine. Garnish with a lemon twist. Though Hemingway would write "drink three to five of these slowly," we actually don't recommend following his advice about alcohol consumption. Drink one in the afternoon and see how you feel.

Brandy Champagne Crusta

1 ½ oz. brandy or cognac

½ oz. Pierre Ferrand dry curacao

½ oz. lemon juice

1 dash Angostura or cinnamon bitters

Sparkling wine, to top

Garnish: sugar rim and wide swath of orange peel, placed inside the cocktail glass.

Take a chilled coupe glass and put a sugar rim around it (that's right, now we're really getting fancy). Set the wide swath of orange peel in a circle inside the coupe glass. Combine everything except the sparkling wine in a mixing glass filled with ice and stir until well chilled. Strain into a coupe or flute glass and top with plenty of good sparkling wine.

Classic Champagne Cocktail

1 sugar cube

2–3 dashes Angostura or cinnamon bitters

Sparkling wine, to top

Garnish: lemon twist

This is one simple cocktail where the sugar cube actually adds to the experience of drinking the cocktail, as little pieces of the sugar cube slowly float to the top of the drink as you enjoy it. In the bottom of a coupe or flute glass, add the sugar cube and soak it with a few dashes of the bitters. Top with sparkling wine and garnish with a lemon twist.

Meyer Lemon Oleo Saccharum

1 cup Meyer lemon peels, washed, scrubbed, and dried

1 cup sugar

Using a vegetable peeler, remove the rinds from the lemons, leaving behind as much of the white pith as possible. Transfer the lemon peels to a medium mixing bowl, add the sugar, and toss to combine. Gently muddle the mixture to help infuse the ingredients. Cover and refrigerate for 48 hours.

Strain the oleo saccharum through a fine-mesh sieve into a clean pint canning jar and discard the solids. Wipe the rim and threads clean, place the lid and ring on, tighten the ring, and refrigerate. Tightly covered, the oleo saccharum will keep for up to 3 weeks in the refrigerator.

Add a teaspoon of this flavor-boosting cocktail ingredient to any of the aforementioned cocktails for an extra kick of citrus oil and aroma. Making oleo and putting it in cocktails is basically cheating, but since there are few rules in drinking, we suggest you do it!

Booze News CHAMPAGNE

BATHING IN CHAMPAGNE IS FROWNED UPON?

One of the strangest yet happiest moments in my life was when a local hustler bought me a bottle of Dom Perignon for my twenty-ninth birthday, at the nightclub where I worked at the time. While I acknowledged the gesture and was very thankful, I felt the best way to share the bottle with my friends was to shower them and myself in hundreds of dollars of wine. As I shook and sprayed the most expensive water gun, drunk on irony, strangers eyed me with disgust at my blatant disrespect for what many consider a beverage of the aristocracy.

Oddly, it would be years before I would hear the legend of former Rolling Stones saxophonist Bobby Keys, who had already one-upped my birthday blast almost forty years earlier. While on the Rolling Stones 1973 fall tour of the United Kingdom and western Europe, Keys would abruptly leave the tour, in Frankfurt, Germany. Following an incident in Belgium the night before, Mr. Keys filled a bathtub with countless bottles of Dom Perignon from their hotel's cellar. According to the Rolling Stones' guitarist Keith Richards, "Bobby Keys is the only man who knows how many bottles it takes to fill a bath, because that's what he was floating in." Keys's entire paycheck from the September and October tour barely covered the wine bill. Even though he was Keith Richards's best friend, it was over ten years before he would rejoin the band.

ICE CREAM MANWICH

Food science pioneer and owner of Lick Me I'm Delicious Ice Cream, Charlie Harry Francis, once admitted to signing a confidentiality agreement to prepare a Viagra-laced, Champagne-flavored ice cream for an "A-List" client.

THIS IS HOW YOU'LL REMEMBER NEW YEAR'S

To encourage responsible transportation during New Year's Eve in Canada's Prince Edward Island, the Kensington PD adopted a strategy—more of a threat—to play Nickelback in the squad car following DUI arrests.

EASY
CLASSIC
BLOODY
MARY
p. 371

FOURTEEN

Settling the Bloody Mary, and Other Hangover Remedies

Social media killed the Bloody Mary,
and yet it lives on . . .

No matter how many towering infernos of fried-food wizardry can be concocted to topple the previous winner of "most outlandish Bloody Mary garnish," none will ever be strong enough to completely cancel the Bloody's staying power. One reason is that the Bloody Mary is one of the only drinks that can help you deal with a hangover while slowly bringing you back to the party. No other drink can lay claim to having so much water-retaining sodium to help your dehydrated body come back to life, while also tasting like a healthful, peppery tonic of fresh vegetables. Throw in hot sauce and vodka? No wonder they are drunk by the thousands every weekend morning in America. But can they actually cure a hangover? A friend of mine once said "the Bloody Mary is a good thing to start with in the morning because it kills hangover breath. It makes your mouth smell like a farmers' market." I'm not sure about that logic, but there is some murky science behind the idea. In Adam Roger's great book *Proof: The Science of Booze*, there is a hypothesis surrounding the idea that a hangover is really just methanol toxicity. Since booze contains trace amounts of methanol, which the body converts to toxic formaldehyde, if you have too much, your body is simply having a toxicity problem. By having that first Bloody Mary at brunch with the pals, you're entering alcohol's main element—ethanol—back into the equation, which helps to cancel out the over-abundance of methanol tracing through your body. What we need to dispel is the notion that the Bloody Mary needs to come with a fried chicken and shrimp skewer, a pickle mold of Guy Fieri's face, a High Life pony, and a slider.

Just as brunch can never really be killed when it comes to being the silent survivor of the restaurant business, a bad hangover can't really be "cured." The only real hangover cure is time spent not drinking (cue the Debbie Downer music). But since we're so far into this book and we've given you a *lot* of delicious recipes to imbibe, it's only fair for us to arm you with some techniques and recipes for those times when you wake up feeling like death is washing over you, or you're lying there silently wishing it was.

Easy Classic Bloody Mary

Serves 2

- 8 oz. tomato juice
- 1 oz. lemon juice
- ½ oz. agave nectar
- 8 dashes Worcestershire sauce
- 8 dashes hot sauce
- 1 teaspoon sea salt
- 1 tablespoon freshly cracked black pepper
- 1 teaspoon celery seeds
- 3-4 oz. vodka, or other spirit you have on hand
- Garnish: celery or parsley

Combine all ingredients in a blender to incorporate, or use an immersion (stick) blender to mix together. Serve over ice in a tall glass with a little pepper cracked over the top.

Batched-out Bloody Mary recipe

For Christmas or New Year's Morning

THE DRY MIX:

2 tablespoons celery seed

3 teaspoons onion powder

3 teaspoons salt

4 teaspoons black pepper

4 teaspoons smoked paprika

½ teaspoon Accent (MSG)

1 teaspoon dill weed

1 teaspoon dried bay leaf powder

1 teaspoon cayenne pepper

Add 3 quarts V8 and the dry mix to a container, and add:

2 cups red wine vinegar

1 cup lemon juice

1 cup lime juice

2 cups Worcestershire sauce

1 cup horseradish (preferably hot horseradish)

2 cups maple syrup or agave

3 cups hot sauce

3 cups water

Whisk like crazy for a while. Add a few more dashes cayenne.

Whisk all this together and taste to see if it's hot enough. Grind 8 turns of black pepper and keep whisking for a while. Taste for heat/ spice level. Serve with plenty of celery and pickled vegetables on a stick.

Way Too Complicated Bloody Mary Mix: The Fancied out Healthy-ish Bloody Mary

Makes 2 quarts

6 oz. chopped celery

3½ oz. chopped sweet onion

3½ oz. chopped peeled carrots

1½ oz. chopped peeled red beets

2 oz. chopped romaine lettuce

2 oz. chopped watercress

1 oz. chopped flat-leaf parsley

4¼ cups tomato juice

⅔ cup fresh lemon juice

½ cup Worcestershire sauce, preferably Bourbon Barrel Worcestershire Sauce

½ cup preserved tomatoes or whole canned tomatoes, with their juices

⅓ cup hot sauce

3 tablespoons agave nectar

2 tablespoons pickling liquid from pickled okra

2 tablespoons apple cider vinegar (optional: infused with hot peppers)

2½ tablespoons prepared horseradish

2 teaspoons kosher salt

1 teaspoon celery seed

¾ teaspoon freshly ground black pepper

¾ teaspoon bourbon smoked paprika

½ teaspoon onion powder

Because the vegetables juice differently than the leafy greens, juice them separately. Combine the celery, onion, carrot, and beet, and run through a juicer. Transfer the juice to a 3-quart container with a lid. Combine the romaine, watercress, and parsley, run through a juicer, and combine with the celery-juice mixture. Add the remaining ingredients, and blend with a handheld immersion blender until smooth, about 1 minute. Cover and refrigerate. Tightly covered, the mix will keep for up to 3 days in the refrigerator.

Mexican Coke and Bitters Drink

½ oz. Angostura bitters

Tiny pinch of salt

Dash of cinnamon

1 orange peel, for garnish

1 bottle of Mexican coke (made with real cane sugar)

Combine the bitters, salt, cinnamon and orange peel at the bottom of a tall glass. Lightly muddle the orange peel with the other ingredients. Add ice. Pour in the coke and stir to combine.

Dr. Pick-Me-Up

by Jessica Backhus

This drink was born from the desire to create an energizing elixir that also served as a non-alcoholic hangover cure for our Husk staff after we all discovered The Batter's Box—a dive bar in the best sense of the word—located a mere 200 yards from the side door to our bar.

When I started working at Husk, I became fascinated with the histories of our ingredients and offerings, especially the story of Dr. Enuf, the Southern soda made with caffeine and B vitamins originally created to energize a sluggish work force. When I started experimenting with it in cocktails, I noticed that iced coffee nicely balanced the sweetness of Dr. Enuf and added an extra punch of caffeine to help shake off aches of the head and limbs.

When I lived in Northern California, my favorite coffee shop served their iced coffee over coffee ice cubes, which I thought was brilliant; and I wondered for years why no one else ever jumped on this innovation. I also realized a coffee cube was a great way to float the iced coffee over the top of the Dr. Pick-Me-Up and create the layering effect. And as the cube melts, it evolves the flavors of the drink, imparting a touch more bitterness with every few sips—the softer start and stronger finish makes it more palatable for someone with a tender tummy; though I firmly believe the more quickly you drink the pick-me-up, the faster it works. In the interest of health and wellness, honey and lime are added for even more vitamins (and to ward off scurvy, the kind you'd get in a dive bar), while the mint settles the stomach. The soda water lightens it up and allows you to taste all these different ingredients working in harmony. Between the medicinal qualities of Dr. Enuf to cure certain ailments, and the caffeine to help you get on with your day, I give you . . .

The Dr. Pick-Me-Up

1½ oz. Dr. Enuf soda (hint for hunting: try your local Cracker Barrel or substitute Sprite)

1½ oz. sparkling water

1 tablespoon fresh lime juice

1 tablespoon Mint Cordial (recipe follows)

1 tablespoon Orange Blossom Honey Syrup (equal parts orange blossom honey and water, stirred to combine)

1 large Coffee Ice Cube (recipe follows)

½ oz. cold-brew coffee

Combine all the ingredients except for the cold-brew coffee in a Canadian whiskey glass or rocks glass, and stir until well chilled. Float the cold-brew coffee on top of the drink, and serve.

Additional notes:

+ In the absence of a glencairn glass, I think a rocks glass is ideal, or a wine/spritz glass works well.

+ I have played with the idea of putting a dash of Angostura (or Fee's Aromatic if you want to keep it truly non-alc) in each of the coffee cubes as they go into the tray to melt; Angostura bitters and coffee is delicious, taking the evolution of the drink in the glass to the next level.

Mint Cordial

Makes 3½ cups

2 cups sugar

1½ cups water

1 cup mint leaves

2 mint sprigs without their leaves

Combine the sugar and water in a small saucepan, and bring the mixture to a simmer over medium heat, stirring to dissolve the sugar. Continue to simmer the syrup for an additional 10 minutes to further thicken the syrup. Transfer to a container, and cool to room temperature. Add the mint leaves and sprigs, cover, and refrigerate for 2 days.

Strain the cordial through a fine-mesh sieve into a clean quart canning jar, and discard the solids. Wipe the rim and threads clean, place the lid and ring on, tighten the ring, and refrigerate. Tightly covered, the cordial will keep for up to 2 weeks in the refrigerator.

Coffee Ice Cube

Makes one 2-inch-square ice cube

4¼ oz. cold-brew coffee

2-inch x 2-inch silicone ice cube mold

Pour the coffee into the ice cube mold and freeze solid. Use the ice cube within 2 days of freezing to prevent it from picking up off-flavors from the freezer.

Booze News HANGOVERS

PUT ENOUGH DEER ANTLER IN SOMETHING, AND . . .

One of the more fascinating, short-lived hangover tonics came about in seventeenth-century England. Goddard Dropps, named after Oliver Cromwell's personal physician and professor at Gresham College and a Warden of Merton College in Oxford, was the product of pulverized and distilled human skulls, dehydrated viper snakes, deer horn, and ivory. Administered for the treatment of bladder stones, fainting, strokes, and a litany of other ailments, Goddard Dropps were quite popular despite having little to no scientific evidence supporting their efficacy. It is speculated, however, that the natural presence of ammonium chloride in deer antlers may have given the tonic a property similar to that of smelling salts.

MAN SPENDS DECADE RESEARCHING HANGOVERS

Toronto-based writing professor and former bar owner Shaughnessy Bishop-Stall spent ten years researching the best way to combat a hangover. Not surprisingly, this took a *lot* of drinking on Bishop-Stall's part. To discover what worked for him on his cure-all quest, he wrote down nearly everything he drank for a decade, while trying out different hangovers along the way. His methods included tried-and-not-so-true techniques such as eating eels and pickled lamb, drinking Bloody Marys, and taking vitamins. Bishop-Stall turned this journey into a book (such a shameless endeavor) called *Hungover: The Morning After and One Man's Quest for the Cure* (Penguin Random House). In the book, he tells of his magic formula, developed through countless days of drinking: a high dose of an amino acid called N-acetylcysteine (NAC), which helps the body make a substantial anti-oxidant called glutathione, which would be a great stoner metal band name.

Gaining notoriety for its use in hospitals to treat Tylenol overdoses, NAC, combined with B vitamins, frankincense, and milk thistle (also containing glutathione), seemed to give Bishop-Stall his best results. As reported in the *New York Post* in December 2018, gastroenterologist Dr. Edward Goldberg thought these claims seemed dubious. "These supplements . . . are more for a chronic alcoholic with liver damage, not a casual drinker with a hangover," said Dr. Goldberg in a fit of rationality. While herbs like milk thistle help with health issues associated with alcoholism, Goldberg noted, "The liver does not cause a hangover, dehydration does." He favors proactive hydration decisions like Pedialyte and coconut water. We in the newsroom wonder why doctors have to be so preachy all the time, sheesh.

I STAND WITH LEMONADE

The ultimate festival drink, perfect large-gathering drink, and still a great way to make money having your kids hawk lemonade:

Infused Lemonade Recipe

3 quarts + 1 cup cold water

2 cups sugar

1¾ cups fresh lemon juice

1 teaspoon kosher salt

½ cup lemon peel, white pith removed

1 large lemon (about 4 oz.), cut into ¼-inch rounds or wheels

2 cups blueberries, blackberries, or sliced strawberries, peaches, or a mix of the three

1½ sprigs mint

1 sprig rosemary

½ sprig thyme

¼ cup lemon balm leaves

¼ cup lemon verbena leaves

1½ large basil leaves

Garnish: blueberries, lemon balm, and basil leaves (all optional)

Combine the water, sugar, lemon juice, and salt in a container large enough to hold all the ingredients, and whisk to dissolve the sugar and salt. Add the lemon peel, lemon rounds, berries, and peaches, and whisk again to help release the flavors from the lemon peel and fruits. Add the remaining ingredients, and whisk just to combine. Cover and refrigerate overnight, or up to 3 days for a more intense herbaceous flavor.

Strain the lemonade through a fine-mesh sieve into a pitcher, and discard the solids (feel free to snack on the berries). Cover and refrigerate in the pitcher until ready to serve. Tightly covered, the lemonade will keep for up to 3 days in the refrigerator.

To complete, pour a tall glass of lemonade and garnish with a few berries and fresh herbs, if desired.

Booze News CITRUS

CITRUS

In the northern Italian town of Ivrea, the Battle of the Oranges Festival has symbolized the proletariat's unity against tyranny, or whatever. Celebrated on the Sunday, Monday, and Tuesday before Ash Wednesday and the beginning of Lent, the BOTO kicks off with Europe's largest food fight. Many dress in medieval costumes; the smart ones wear helmets, it's that brutal. In 2016, the opening ceremony attracted 7,000 to the fight, with 16,000 spectators lining the streets. By day's end, the casualties tallied 70 concussions related to bombardment of orange and slippage. Another 28 were hospitalized for alcohol poisoning.

Booze News LEMONADE

LEMONADE

Country Time, owned by Kraft foods, once established a charity to help children pay fines for operating unlicensed lemonade stands.

FLY JANUARY: NON-ALCOHOLIC DRINKS

Celery Shrub

1 pint diced celery, as local as you can get it

1 pint organic sugar

1 pint distilled white vinegar

1 oz. lemon juice

¼ cup loosely packed parsley leaves

1 tablespoon celery seeds

Place the diced celery in a sterilized container and add the sugar on top. Let the mixture sit in the fridge for a few days, then add the rest of the ingredients and whisk to combine. Return the mixture to the refrigerator and let it infuse for a week, checking it for strength after 3 to 4 days. When you're happy with the flavor, strain, bottle, and store in the refrigerator for up to 2 months.

Celery Tonic

4 quarts water

1 rib diced celery, with tops

2 cups celery root, peeled and chopped

2 cups parsley, roughly chopped

2 cups honey

1 cup distilled white vinegar

In a pot, bring the water to a boil, then lower the heat to a hard simmer, add the diced celery and celery root, and cook for 20 minutes. Next, add the parsley and lower the heat to a low simmer. Let the ingredients simmer together for 30 to 45 minutes, covered. Add the honey to your tonic and stir to incorporate. Strain, cool, and add the vinegar. Serve the tonic hot or enjoy over ice. This mixture will keep in the fridge, covered, for one week.

Fennel Cordial

2 cups sugar

1 cup water

½ large fennel bulb (about 8 oz.), fronds removed and chopped and bulb thinly sliced

3 tablespoons grated lime zest (use a Microplane)

Combine the sugar, water, fennel fronds, and fennel bulb in a medium saucepan and bring the mixture to a simmer over medium heat, stirring to dissolve the sugar, about 5 minutes. Remove from the stove and add the lime zest, sprinkling it on top of the cooling cordial.

Cool the cordial to room temperature, transfer to a clean jar, wipe the rim and threads clean, place the lid and ring on, tighten the ring, and let the cordial infuse for 2 days in the refrigerator.

Strain the cordial through a fine-mesh sieve into a clean quart canning jar, and discard the solids. Wipe the rim and threads clean, place the lid and ring on, tighten the ring, and refrigerate. Tightly covered, the cordial will keep for up to 2 weeks in the refrigerator.

ACKNOWLEDGMENTS

We'd like to thank our producer Michael Eades and everyone at the We Own This Town Podcast Network for helping to spread the Liquid Gold gospel over the years. Thanks to Ryan Smernoff, Todd Bottorff, Lauren Ash, and everyone at Turner Publishing for their support and patience in getting this book out into the world. Thank you Stephanie Bowman for believing in us and helping immeasurably in getting this project off the ground. A million thank you's to photographer Christine Souder, whose beautiful work made this book a joy to look at. And thank you to Jess Machen who has always done such great artwork for Liquid Gold!

Thanks to my lovely wife, Kate, for her support in all my writing endeavors and for making me the occasional martini when I needed it. Thanks to my amazing children, Leila and Henry, for giving me so much joy and making me laugh at all times. Thanks to my parents, Mark and Cheryl, for always making the holidays so special around the house and for helping me get across the finish line with this book. To Cathy and Don Barnett for hosting incredible family dinners over the years. Thanks to my brother Matt for his Thanksgiving brussels sprouts and for always cooking amazing food during the holidays. Thanks also to Lisa, Anabelle, Frank Pryor, Matt Campbell, Sherri and Roger, Marilyn, Siobhan and Alison, John and Dana, Kim and Reggie, Marianne and Dave, Cassie Berman, Inglewood Public Library, Sam Jett, Sean Brock and the whole team at Audrey, the Bookshop East, Parnassus Books, the Tattered Cover, Rory, Adam, Amie and everyone at Husk, Kenny Lyons, Kevin King and Vilda Gonzalez, Todd and Suzanne Flohr, Cooper and Marie Rainey, Jonathan Howard, Victoria Koronkiewicz, Hope Rice, Adam Roberts, Adam Schreiber, Jodi Bronchtein, Mars Mayer, Kaytie Keck, Jessica, Aimee, Kathy and Rich Rutkowski, John and Kali Souder and family, Bob and Ashley Souder and the epic holiday dinners at your house, Stephen Polcz, Patrick Goodspeed, Upright T Rex, Lisa Donovan,

Amy Stewart, and Alice Randall. Thank you so much to illustrator Jenna Pearl Leonard, who added so much whimsy and beauty to this book with her artwork, Jenna, you're a joy to work with.

Thanks to contributors Kenneth Dedmon, Jessica Backhus, and Brittany Augustine for enriching this project with their writing, wit, and wisdom. I'm fortunate to work with all of you!

ABOUT THE AUTHOR

Mike Wolf is a writer, bar manager, vermouth maker, broadcaster, gardener, husband, and father living in Nashville, Tennessee. He opened and established the bar program at Husk in Nashville, spending five years developing a hyper-seasonal and regional approach to cocktails, commemorated in his first book, *Garden to Glass: Grow Your Drinks from the Ground Up*, hailed by Paste magazine as the "best food or drink book of 2019." He opened the tropical drinks and robot tiki haven Chopper in East Nashville in summer 2019. His second book, *Barantined*, a culmination of recipes and stories from bartenders around the country dealing with a global pandemic, came out in spring 2021. He co-hosts the podcast, *Liquid Gold*, which is the partial namesake of this book, along with co-contributors and Booze News anchor Kenneth Dedmon and Cocktail Correspondent Jessica Backhus. Wolf has been making vermouth with Love and Exile Wines in Nashville and is currently the bar manager at Sean Brock's new flagship restaurant, Audrey.

Printed in the USA
CPSIA information can be obtained
at www.ICGtesting.com
JSHW071308150823
46574JS00005B/217

9 781684 425631